CONTEMPORARY MONOLOGUES FOR A NEW THEATER

CONTEMPORARY MONOLOGUES FOR A NEW THEATER

EDITED BY CATE CAMMARATA

APPLAUSE
THEATRE & CINEMA BOOKS
AN IMPRINT OF HAL LEONARD LLC

Published in 2018 by Applause Theatre & Cinema Books
An Imprint of Hal Leonard LLC
7777 West Bluemound Road
Milwaukee, WI 53213

Trade Book Division Editorial Offices
33 Plymouth St., Montclair, NJ 07042

Play Sources aned Permissions can be found on pages 195 to 200, which constitute an extension of this copyright page.

Printed in the United States of America

Book design by Lynn Bergesen, UB Communications

Library of Congress Cataloging-in-Publication Data

Names: Cammarata, Cate, editor.
Title: Contemporary monologues for a new theater / edited by Cate Cammarata.
Description: Milwaukee, WI : Applause Theatre & Cinema Books, 2018. |
  Includes bibliographical references.
Identifiers: LCCN 2018005043 | ISBN 9781495069789 (pbk.)
Subjects: LCSH: Monologues. | Acting.
Classification: LCC PN2080 .C64814 2018 | DDC 812/.04508—dc23
LC record available at https://lccn.loc.gov/2018005043

www.applausebooks.com

CONTENTS

Acknowledgments   ix

Introduction   xi

Women's Monologues

After by Glenn Alterman   3

The Sealing of Ceil by Glenn Alterman   5

(O)n the 5:31 by Mando Alvarado   7

Goodnight Lovin' Trail by John Patrick Bray   9

Liner Notes by John Patrick Bray (Alice 1)   11

Liner Notes by John Patrick Bray (Alice 2)   14

Nightmares: A Demonstration of the Sublime
  by Adam R. Burnett   16

The Director by Barbara Cassidy (Sadie)   18

The Director by Barbara Cassidy (Nina)   20

The Director by Barbara Cassidy (Annie)   22

Iowa of My Mind by Barbara Cassidy (Chloe)   24

Iowa of My Mind by Barbara Cassidy (Samantha 1)   25

Iowa of My Mind by Barbara Cassidy (Samantha 2)   27

Out of Focus by Geralyn Cassidy (Happy 1)   29

Out of Focus by Geralyn Cassidy (Happy 2)   31

The Demon Hunter by Nat Cassidy   34

Row After Row by Jessica Dickey   37

Sister Cities by Colette Freedman (Carolina)   41

Sister Cities by Colette Freedman (Mary)   44

Sister Cities by Colette Freedman (Dallas)   48

Sister Cities by Colette Freedman (Austin)   50

Sister Cities by Colette Freedman (Baltimore)   52

E-Mail: 9/12 by Midge Guerrara (Sergeant Ally M. Forte)   54

E-Mail: 9/12 by Midge Guerrara (Marilyn)   58

E-Mail: 9/12 by Midge Guerrara (Miriam)   60

Our Lady of Kibeho by Katori Hall   62

Marly Florinda Descends Into Hell One Step at a Time
    by Anne Hamilton   64

OFEM by Anne Hamilton   67

Going Up by Penny Jackson   70

See Something, Say Something by Penny Jackson   73

St. Francis by Miranda Jonte (Tessa 1)   78

St. Francis by Miranda Jonte (Tessa 2)   80

St. Francis by Miranda Jonte (Tessa 3)   82

The Rise and Fall of a Teenage Cyber Queen by Lindsay Joy   85

Last Call by Kelly McAllister   88

Muse of Fire by Kelly McAllister   90

Some Unfortunate Hour by Kelly McAllister   91

Breeders by Bob Ost   93

The Fortification of Miss Grace Wren by Robin Rice   95

Queen for a Day by Robin Rice   97

Mala Hierba by Tanya Saracho   99

Elephant by Margie Stokley   102

Pretty Theft by Adam Szymkowicz (Suzy)   104

Pretty Theft by Adam Szymkowicz (Allegra 1)   106

Pretty Theft by Adam Szymkowicz (Allegra 2)   108

Rare Birds by Adam Szymkowicz   110

When January Feels Like Summer by Cori Thomas   113

Arrangements by Ken Weitzman   115

The Ask by David Lee White   117

Men's Monologues

After by Glenn Alterman   123

Nobody's Flood by Glenn Alterman   125

With a Bullet (or, Surprise Me) by John Patrick Bray   127

Liner Notes by John Patrick Bray (George 1)   129

Liner Notes by John Patrick Bray (George 2)   132

Nightmares: A Demonstration of the Sublime
by Adam R. Burnett   134

Iowa of My Mind by Barbara Cassidy   139

Our Lady of Kibeho by Katori Hall   141

An Octoroon by Branden Jacobs-Jenkins   145

Herman Kline's Midlife Crisis by Josh Koenigsberg   148

North to Maine by Brenton Lengel   150

The Country House by Donald Margulies   152

Burning the Old Man by Kelly McAllister   154

Last Call by Kelly McAllister   157

Some Unfortunate Hour by Kelly McAllister (Tom 1)   159

Some Unfortunate Hour by Kelly McAllister (Tom 2)   161

Sitting Duck Season by Robin Rice   163

House of Trash by Trav S.D.   165

Not to Be Negative But . . . by Jack Sundmacher (Jack 1)   168

Not to Be Negative But . . . by Jack Sundmacher (Jack 2)   171

Pretty Theft by Adam Szymkowicz (Bobby)   174

Pretty Theft by Adam Szymkowicz (Joe)   177

Rare Birds by Adam Szymkowicz (Evan Wills 1)   179

Rare Birds by Adam Szymkowicz (Evan Wills 2)   181

When January Feels Like Summer by Cori Thomas
     (Devaun)   183

When January Feels Like Summer by Cori Thomas (Joe)   186

When January Feels Like Summer by Cori Thomas
     (Jeron)   188

The As if Body Loop by Ken Weitzman   191

Credits and Permissions   195

ACKNOWLEDGMENTS

Editing a collection of monologues like this one is just as collaborative as the art of theater itself, and almost as rewarding! But, as we all know, it is the communal effort and generosity of so many dedicated artists that go into creating a book like this one.

First, I have to thank all of my talented and gracious playwrights. The playwright community has been extremely warm and welcoming to this idea, and I have met many talented artists through this endeavor that I wouldn't have met otherwise. I look forward to working with them more as time goes on, for they are as generous and bighearted as they are talented. I hope that this collection opens their work up to much more study and many more productions. Thank you for allowing me to publish your scripts.

There are not enough words to thank Martin and Rochelle Denton for their dedication and service to the indie theater community. I first met Rochelle in the back of the Judson Memorial Church gym. I was alone, and Rochelle's easy and gracious manner made me feel like an old friend by the time the show was over. Both Martin and Rochelle worked tirelessly for almost two decades to bring Off-Off-Broadway reviews and information to the NYC public through the Internet and their private publishing company. Rochelle was able to help track down every writer that I couldn't find so that they could be included in this collection—an example of their commitment to the Off-Off-Broadway community. I am indebted to them as a theater artist, professor, producer, writer, and friend.

I want to thank Bob Ost, the executive director, president, and founder of Theater Resources Unlimited, for suggesting me as a potential editor. Like Martin and Rochelle, Bob has spent his life serving the NYC theater community. Bob knows everyone in theater in this town and remembers every detail about each. A true artist and dedicated friend, he has launched many producers' careers through his nonprofit organization, whose mission is to "help producers produce." I am beyond grateful for his belief in me and helping me launch my career both as a producer and now as a writer.

Finally, I'd like to thank my editor, Carol Flannery, for all of her support and her patience with me on this journey. Thank you, Carol, for all of your help. I'm so happy that you took the chance!

INTRODUCTION

In my classes with university students at Stony Brook University, on the first day of the semester I will ask them a big question: "Why did you sign up for this theater course? Why are you here?" The answer given 90 percent of the time is something along the lines of "I needed an art course to fulfill my core requirements, and this fit in my schedule." One young student athlete was more blunt: "My advisor forced me to take this."

Ouch.

Ninety percent of the time, my non-theater-major college students simply enroll in my classes hoping to get that "easy A." Sometimes I will get lucky. I'll see a few students who were active in their high school drama clubs, or some aspiring screenwriter will join because, well, the cinema studies courses didn't fit into his schedule. But most often, the largest number, remembering that my classes are always filled to capacity with fifty students, tell me that they never really see theater at all. It never occurs to them to see a play when their lives are full of YouTube, concerts, movies, social media, and PlayStation.

Why is that? And as theater people, what can we do about it? Is theater still relevant in this new century?

By the end of our semester, I poll my students again. I ask, "Is theater relevant? Is it useful to society?" And this time, having spent three months exploring contemporary artists and theater companies *and* having created their own devised performances, my students will answer a resounding *yes*. *Yes* because they have participated in creating and staging their own visions. *Yes* because they are on fire with their own creative imaginations and addicted to the sense of "family" that always surrounds a group with common goals. And *yes* because they've participated in that ageless collaborative process that shares their own perspectives and pain and experiences and a bit of their hearts and souls with other people in the context of a live performance.

This vision is caught, not taught. Contemporary theater is alive, vibrant, and vital to our culture. Its role is to hold a mirror up to society and manipulate the mirror so that audiences can see hidden reflections in the shadows and the refracted colors and sounds dancing in plain sight. Theater creates a path of empathy, as it always has, by engaging an audience in the story, investing them emotionally in the journey of the characters and thus having them emerge from the theater somehow changed by the entire experience. We are admonished not to judge a man until we walk a mile in his shoes; audiences walk a mile and then some every time they see a play. It is as true today even as it was for the Greeks— theater makes us more fully human.

I've compiled these monologues in the hope that actors and readers alike will walk a mile in these characters' shoes and emerge with a greater depth of understanding, on many different levels, of the plurality of life experience in the United States at the turn of the twenty-first century. We live in unique times, and I believe future generations will look back and see our era as undergoing as massive and all-encompassing a change as how we view the end of the nineteenth century and the industrial age, or the twentieth century and the political fallout from two world wars.

But we're not historians; we're artists. We want to know the human experience. We want to know how individuals charted their way through difficult times. How they woke up every day and coped. We want to be amazed at the human spirit and inspired to endure our own tough times.

Read on. I've been honored to collect almost one hundred human experiences, or monologues, that expose our hopes and fears, our bravado and our masks, as we live life at the turn of this new millennium. By performing these monologues and, hopefully, reading the entire plays, you will emerge with a better understanding of the diversity and the beauty of life on this planet at this point in human history. You will hopefully emerge with more empathy toward those with different perspectives because you've walked a mile in their shoes, through this art of theater that we all love. Passionately. And, if we need anything today as a nation, we need empathy.

Do you think theater is relevant? I hope your answer will be a resounding *yes*.

WOMEN'S MONOLOGUES

AFTER

Glenn Alterman

CHARACTER: TERRY, middle-aged, bubbly

PLACE: A stage

CIRCUMSTANCE: Talking to the audience about her dead husband.

TERRY (*Smiling.*): Sidney and me, we were married nearly thirty-two years, yeah. And let me tell you, you couldn't ask for a better husband. Except, well, he was—gay. We never really talked about it, but, well, he knew I knew. A *wink* every once in a while. Times were different back then; there was no need to talk about things like that. 'Sides, why ruin a good thing, right? And let me tell ya, I *loved* being his wife. Every day with Sidney was a blessing. He was a good, caring man.

Anyway, I feel people talk too much today. I hate all those stupid talk shows, people always needing to reveal every . . . Sometimes what really matters . . . It's the *not* saying, y'know? The things people don't need to say to each other. The, I don't know, *unspoken*, that's most meaningful.

(*A slight sadness.*) I miss him, yeah. Sidney was my . . . He was more than just my husband, he was my *companion*. Friends and lovers, eh, they come and go. But a *companion*, that's someone so special, someone who's always there for you. And we went everywhere together, traveled, did everything. We loved being in each other's company, made each other laugh. Incredible; lucky, love.

THE SEALING OF CEIL

Glenn Alterman

CHARACTER: CEIL, a lonely housewife, in her thirties to fifties

PLACE: An apartment in New York City

CIRCUMSTANCE: Speaking to her friend Fran about her affair.

CEIL: I went for a walk. Just a few blocks, Times Square. Felt I needed to get out of here. Sometimes I do that, go over there to clear my head, "escape." I was thinking . . . Oh, I don't know what the hell I was thinking. Just went, walked, looked at all the people. It's Wednesday, y'know, matinee day, crowds, tourists. Was lunchtime, so I figured I'd get a bit to eat. Stopped off somewhere, some bar on Eighth Avenue. But I realized I really wasn't hungry, so I ordered a drink, a *vodka*; vodka and tonic. Sat at the bar, sipped it. When this man came in, sat down right next to me, next stool. He smiled, I nodded; he said hello. Said his name was Hank. Very handsome, nice eyes, eyes that look right through ya. We sat there, talked about I don't remember what. Then out of the blue, he told me how pretty I looked. I smiled, wanted to say, "C'mon, Hank, look like I was born yesterday? Thanks for the compliment but who you kiddin'?"

(*Softly.*) But I just sat there, ate it up, let him continue. Let his compliments rain on me like some waterfall. He was looking right at me, *really* looking. I mean all that attention, Fran. It felt . . .

Was like it was just the two of us there, all alone, no one else, y'know? And soon he seemed, I don't know, desirable. And I thought, "What the hell you thinking?! You outta your mind?! You're married. Mike! What are you doing?! Mike would . . . !

I turned to Hank, asked him if he wanted to come home with me. Told him I only lived a few blocks away. Told him I was *interested*. He smiled, stood up, said, "Sure." Just like that. "Sure."

(*Accelerating.*) We left, started to walk, slow at first, but then faster. Neither of us said a word. Just kept walking—faster, faster! Blocks flew by. Passing people, stores. Walking even faster, rushing! Realized, I realized, I didn't know anything about him, nothing, just his name! Faster, faster! Finally, we got to the building here. The door downstairs flew open! We ran up the stairs, key in, opened the door, and . . . and well . . . that's how it began.

(O)N THE 5:31

Mando Alvarado

CHARACTER: GINA MORGAN, twenties to early forties

PLACE: A room

CIRCUMSTANCE: Speaking to Benny, who takes on the shape of all her ex-boyfriends.

GINA: You wanna know the last time I felt really happy with you?

(BENNY: *When?*)

GINA: I came across this short story. About a lady who lived in the country or some farm or something. And every morning, her husband would take the train into the city for work. One of those mornings, she was watching the news and she saw that there had been a train wreck. No survivors. The train was the 5:31 . . . her husband's train. A flood of *relief* came over her. Not sadness, relief! And she started dancing around her living room, dreaming of all the things she would do—now her life would really begin! Then the doorbell rings. She opens it. And standing there is her husband. Sadness washes over her and she begins to sob. He assumed it was for him, for being lucky he didn't get on the 5:31. But it was for herself. For the death of her soul. And I think about that. About her. And then I think about you, Juan—

(BENNY: *Larry*—)

GINA: Jim, I think about you. And what you're doing to me. Killing my soul. And I imagine that you were on that train. And that thought. Your body smashed to pieces. Limbs ripped apart. Face mangled, unrecognizable. That brings a small smile to my face. Because I have my soul back. Just for a moment. Do you understand what I'm saying to you?

(BENNY: *You're a real bitch.***)**

GINA: I need you to get on the five fucking thirty-one.

GOODNIGHT LOVIN' TRAIL

John Patrick Bray

CHARACTER: LEE, late twenties-thirties, a waitress

PLACE: A dying diner in a rural American small town

CIRCUMSTANCE: Lee is talking to Mr. Coffee and Cigarettes, a drifting guitar player. Mr. Coffee believes that Lee may have stolen his guitar to pawn while he was outside, passed out drunk. In his attempt to get her to confess to stealing and hiding the guitar, he accidentally gets her to confess to killing her husband.

LEE: He didn't check out—I killed him!

(*Beat.*)

I said what I said. Yes, sir. I was never gonna tell no one, but YOU, going on and on about the ocean and shit, and scars—!

(*Beat.*)

Feel so bad?! He fuckin' got it! He hit the children, see. He hit them hard. When Austin was five years old, just five, he walks over and strikes him so hard upside the head, Austin ends up saying nothing for three whole years. Each second, I'm waiting. I know he'll come around, I know it. Then the old man starts hitting baby Sarah. And I can't take it. I ask my son on a rainy night in June what to do, what to do, and he stares at me. Others might say that he isn't there, but I can see him screaming in his eyes, 'Stop him, Mommy. Do what you can, and stop him.'

So I do.

He's out on the porch, back from hunting. Of course he didn't catch nothing. He sets down his shotgun for a moment, and in that moment, I snatch it up. He doesn't hear me, not at first. I'm not sure if I would really have gone through with it, but he spins around, screaming. It startles me. And that was it. His heart exploded. I even buried him.

I . . . I . . . oh, Lord.

And when I'm done, done, patting down the last of the dirt, crying why, and spitting on the ground, my boy Austin comes up behind me, quiet as a mouse and whispers. 'What have you done, Mommy?'

(*Beat.*)

What have I done?

LINER NOTES

John Patrick Bray

CHARACTER: ALICE, twenty, the daughter of the deceased rock and roll legend Jake Sampson

PLACE: George's apartment in South Carolina. Neat, except for Hungry-Man dinner boxes all over. George, late forties–early fifties, is Jake Sampson's former guitar player.

CIRCUMSTANCE: George sits at his desk, writing on his computer. There is a knock at the door. George would rather not answer. Another knock. George resigns himself and opens the door. Alice enters without looking at him.

ALICE: I meant to bring coffee—

(GEORGE: *Excuse—?*)

ALICE: It's this place I work at—Café Art Java, near the metro station. I'm standing there yesterday morning, about to make coffee, and not just coffee for me, but for everybody, I mean my entire part of town shows up at 5:15, even though we don't open until 5:30, but it's this LUNATIC Annie that works there, she opens the door wide open at 3 a.m., singing her heart out to Bonnie Tyler or worse, Leonard Cohen, letting all the lunatics just hang out, eating cookies free of charge, and so when people show up at 5:15, they expect their coffee to be ready, and she knows all their orders; BUT if SHE'S not working, and I'M working, I don't open the store until 5:30, which is when we open; so, I've got a line by 5:25, people banging, literally BANGING on the glass, pointing to their watches, AND WHAT THE FUCK KIND OF JOBS DO THEY WORK THAT THEY NEED COFFEE BY 5:30? And so, I'm standing, the coffee maker's going, no Bonnie Tyler today, my heart is fucking POUNDING IN MY CHEST, and I can't even look at the book—

(GEORGE:—*the book?*)

ALICE:—and I'm like, FUCK IT! NOBODY GETS COFFEE TODAY! NONE OF YOU GET COFFEE! MONTREAL CAN HAVE A FUCKING LACK-OF-CAFFEINE-INDUCING-MIGRAINE FOR ALL I FUCKING CARE! FUCK YOU AND YOUR COFFEE NEEDS, YOU FUCKING ADDICTS OF FUCKING—GRRRRRRRRRR! And I get my car, they're all looking at me with destroyed coffee-less faces, I might as well have killed a cute puppy and dropped it on their heads for the sulking they're doing, as I'm speeding away . . . and I can't drive home, the carpet needs cleaning, there's dishes, there's MY MOTHER, who, don't worry knows I'm here—

(GEORGE: *She does?*)

ALICE:—and I don't know what to do, so I end up driving here.

(GEORGE: [*Beat.*] *To South Carolina?*)

ALICE: I need to smoke . . . can I smoke in here?

(GEORGE: *No.*)

ALICE: Good. (*Takes out cigarette. Beat.*) Shit. (*Puts down cigarette.*) You sure?

(*He nods.*)

Shit. (*She holds the cigarettes, paces, and throws them.*) Shit!

(*Pause. She bursts into tears. GEORGE watches her, still holding an academic journal.*)

I found your address a few days ago, and I don't know, it just seemed like the only thing to do.

(*Awkward moment. GEORGE looks at his dinner, and picks up a cup of coffee.*)

(**GEORGE:** *Coffee?*)

(*She glares at him.*)

(**GEORGE:** *It's decaf, and it's just as tasty.*)

(*She lets out a big sob. GEORGE moves to touch her hair, but doesn't. ALICE sits on his sofa. GEORGE sits on a chair. He watches her a moment.*)

ALICE: Can I stay the night?

LINER NOTES

John Patrick Bray

CHARACTER: ALICE, twenty, the daughter of the late rock and roll legend Jake Sampson

PLACE: Her father's grave

CIRCUMSTANCE: Alice visits her dad's grave with his estranged friend and former lead guitarist George. Alice needs answers about who her father was, and hopes that George can shed some light on that.

ALICE (*Looking intensely at the grave.*): There were TWO people missing at that funeral, George. You and Jake! I'm standing there, looking at strangers, fans, aging groupies, some woman threw her panties at the grave, George, and I thought it was a fucking PARACHUTE! (*Beat.*) I'm looking around these faces, his fucking sleaze-old agent, a teenage girl that I KNOW he was fucking three nights a week, and my mom, and . . . YOU. WEREN'T. THERE. The two who understood what this fucking death was all about, the one who . . . who died and the one who could decipher that death's meaning, were completely fucking ABSENT! You're his guitarist, DECIPHER! FIGURE IT OUT! HUM IT IF YOU NEED TO! WHAT DOES IT MEAN?! I. DON'T. KNOW. MY. FATHER. HELP ME! PUT YOUR LAPEL UP . . . OR DOWN AND FIGURE IT OUT!

(*Beat.*)

It's what I need, George!

(*She cries. He approaches her, but isn't sure.*)

My dad was more than an asshole, George. Right? Wasn't he?

(*Long pause.*)

And I love you because I want to love you, and I don't know what that means, either, do you?!

(*She holds on to him, sobbing.*)

Please . . . say something. Please . . . (*Beat.*) What makes you different from him?

(GEORGE: *I'm here.*)

ALICE: Oh, God . . . oh, God.

(GEORGE: *Hang on—*)

ALICE: No, no. I . . . I cleaned his blood off the carpet, George. I just got down and started doing it. I can't . . . I can't do that again, you know? (*Beat.*) Hungry-Man? Hating your wife? Jake's last album was ten years ago. When was yours? (*Beat.*) How long until you're staring down the barrel of a gun, huh?!

(*Beat.*)

I changed my mind. I don't want to understand any of it.

(*She throws the joint box at the headstone and rushes off.*)

NIGHTMARES: A DEMONSTRATION OF THE SUBLIME

Adam R. Burnett

CHARACTER: ALLERGIC GIRL

PLACE: A stage

CIRCUMSTANCE: Present time.

ALLERGIC GIRL: There's a camp, at home, called Back 2 Nature. Everyone went *back* to nature. You spent a week *in* nature. We would put up our tent and tarp. The tarp, which had correct usage: that is, it was rendered useless if you put it on the wrong way. The rain, water, would come through, soaking the camping children. Also, there were the beans in cans. Nothing ever tasted very good. The silver dollars were okay, but I always ended up eating tinfoil. Which hurt the teeth. Miserable.

Each field outside the forest would have a different game activity: the soccer field, the kickball field, the field with the rope game. One summer they had a zip line and the mother of some child kept hogging it from the kids: we called her the Silver Back. Because she was big and had silver hair. Whenever the mom went down the zip line, all the kids would make gorilla sounds. She thought we were cheering her on. So she kept doing it.

I remember the bugs and the sweat and getting sick. I would always get sick and have to go home before the end. I'd call my mother and father and they'd say, "What? You don't like camping?"

I'M SICK! It's making me SICK!

Still this way: whenever I spend more than, say, four hours outside, I get sick. I get really ill. I don't feel well, nauseous. It makes me sick to be outside. I'd like to be like, WOW! JESUS CHRIST! ISN'T IT GORGEOUS? ISN'T THIS INCREDIBLE. FUCK, I LOVE IT! But my eyes are so wet and my nose itches and I'm so anxious—the bugs, the bites, the ticks, the disease—THE LYME'S DISEASE. Nothing is pretty. Not when your eyeballs are itching that much.

I found a remedy, though. My boyfriend and I do Google images a lot now: you know, the grand pyramids, the Great Wall, the Amazon. It's okay.

THE DIRECTOR

Barbara Cassidy

CHARACTER: SADIE, a woman working on a project who once knew the Director

PLACE: A bare stage

CIRCUMSTANCE: Sadie sits on the floor of a room. She is surrounded by micro cassette tapes and goes through them while she talks to the audience.

SADIE: I have a lot of tapes here. I'm looking for one that has some information on it.

Something that was said. Nothing seems real right now. Somehow it seems like . . . I don't know . . . It's all in front of me. There is a very surreal nature to the way it is right now. It feels a little like a dream. I'm sure you've had that feeling. Well, everyone has.

So right, well, the idea for the director project . . .

I had met a guy a while back who was really into pursuing women, a lot of women. He was a film director. He would go up to chicks on the street, telling them he was interested in them, that they just had something about them, and that I was making such and such a film, and he would like to talk to them about working in his film. This is the way I met him. It almost sounds too cliché even to believe, right? That there could be someone around doing this kind of thing.

The director is an idea.

I have a really odd feeling right now. I don't feel safe. I feel a presence. I'm sorry. You probably think I'm crazy. Someone I know killed themselves. Shot in the head. Today. I think it was today. That may be why I'm acting a little strange . . . Don't mind me.

I am looking for a tape.

I have him on one of the tapes and he talks about his philosophy of life and all. It is very interesting. I find it stimulating. I do.

I put an ad in the paper for women who were approached by the director and I received a lot of responses. Wait, I think I have it.

"Seeking women who have been approached on the streets of Manhattan by a fairly well-known film director, offering possible film work. I am interested in interviewing women for a theater project I am working on. No compensation."

Milton said I should compensate them. But I didn't think it was a good idea. Because I'm broke. And maybe other reasons. Milton was very weird when I first met her. I'm not sure why. I never asked her.

I interviewed the women. They're in these tapes. Many of them hate him. He propositioned them and never came through with the said parts. Mostly.

I'm not sure if I hate him or not.

THE DIRECTOR

Barbara Cassidy

CHARACTER: NINA, a woman who Sadie interviews who met the Director

PLACE: A bare stage

CIRCUMSTANCE: Speaking to the audience.

NINA: There were a lot of times we were together, but still I would never sleep with him. I knew he really wanted to. He walked around with a hard-on a lot. He would do his little routine with chicks all the time, though, so it wasn't like I was anything special to him. Maybe I just understood him a little more. I think he did it like twenty-five times a day or something, I swear, he just went up to everyone. We would joke about it. You know there's something wrong with a person that has the need to do that. I mean I kind of felt sorry for him. Oh, oh, and then on top of that he had the subway thing, you know about that, right? Yeah, the first time I met him in a coffee shop to talk, he gives me this script, or I think he called it an idea page, the idea page he called it, he gave it to me to read and he says he'll be right back, he's going next door to the subway station to get a map. And I'm like you're what! He had this thing, this obsession with the NY subway system. He was in the process of committing to memory all of the subway lines in the city, each and every station. He thought this would be good information to have. In case the need ever arose. And I'm like you have got to be kidding, man. But he was just in love with the idea of having a subway map in his brain, and that this was the common man's mode of transport and he would know everything about it, and it's funny but he kind of made that sound sexy. Some people can find the interesting element in anything and this is something that I think all the girls clued in to. So you can imagine how obsessed with the subway he had to be if he's slipping this in during a meeting, but then, yeah, when else would he, what with all the girls he's meeting too. I mean, can you imagine giving his come-on twenty times a day or whatever he does. That must get really tired, wouldn't it. It almost seems a bore. I mean, it sounds wild and crazy at first, but I think he's a slave to his compulsions and what a drag that must be.

THE DIRECTOR

Barbara Cassidy

CHARACTER: ANNIE, a woman who Sadie interviews who met the Director

PLACE: A bare stage

CIRCUMSTANCE: Speaking to the audience.

ANNIE: I was walking down the street and it's, I hear this kind of "Hey, hey." And I'm coming from the gym and I feel I think rather, I don't know, frumpy, I feel not very attractive, I say this because I think it's important, I think it has some relevance to my reaction. But anyway, so I hear this "hey, hey" and I don't think it's anybody talking to me, so I keep walking and then I hear this like panting, this guy has run up to me and says, "Hey, can I talk to you a minute." And I'm like c'mon, really? "Ya know I am not up for this bullshit." And I'm walking fast and he starts jogging to keep up with me, which is kind of funny 'cause and it's kind of hard for him to do that and talk. He's totally out of breath; he must smoke. And he is wearing this hat and his face is puffy and he's sweating. He's got to be at least fifty. And he's like let me just talk to you, okay? And I'm like thinking it's funny, okay, what? And he gives me the whole bit about the thinking I have something, and I guess on the one hand I know this is total bullshit, but on the other, here I am feeling like I look like shit and I guess I'm kind of flattered in some odd way. That he picked me. I have to admit that. And I'm sure no matter what the women tell you, that they were somewhat flattered. Even the harassment an attractive woman faces as she walks down the street of NY. I mean, I'm talking about the catcalls from the construction workers and so on, those harassments would be missed or will be missed as she gets older, or if she doesn't look as attractive one day . . . So he's talking and talking and going on and I'm laughing. And in some odd way I'm captivated. I mean, there was something about the way he was, the confidence in the face of his ugliness. Maybe that was it. And I had heard of his films, though I was not all that familiar with them. Then he asks me if he saw my naked body what sport would he think I played. And I'm like you have got to be kidding, guy? And he's like c'mon just answer, what's the big deal? So I thought what is the big deal . . . and said, uh, softball?

IOWA OF MY MIND

Barbara Cassidy

CHARACTER: CHLOE, a woman mid- to late thirties

PLACE: A bare stage

CIRCUMSTANCE: Speaking to the audience.

CHLOE: I am crazy about big old-fashioned breakfasts, you know, scrambled eggs, home fries, toast, bacon, crispy and sizzling. Mmmmm. It makes me feel really content to have one of those. I don't do it every day, I can't, my body would show it. But on Saturday morning, that's my time to let go. Yes, sir! During the week I have yogurt and fruit usually. Sometimes a smoothie, if I'm running out the door and need some nutrition. My kids keep me pretty busy. My bigger one goes to school for a couple of hours in the morning, but I'm spending most of my time doing stuff with them. I signed them up for gymnastics and music class. They seem to enjoy it, but, you know, they're young. I really like kids. I'm not sure what I want to do myself. I went to school for business. I guess I could go back to work at the company I worked for before the kids. Or maybe I could do something on my own, maybe . . . I like books too . . . I have a theory that women who were sexually abused as children wind up very sexually free as adults, they are just very sexy people. They seem very comfortable with sex. I wonder why that is.

IOWA OF MY MIND

Barbara Cassidy

CHARACTER: SAMANTHA, a woman mid- to late thirties

PLACE: A bare stage

CIRCUMSTANCE: Samantha is cleaning, polishing the floor. The kids are not there.

SAMANTHA: Without pause, there is no creation.
An unexamined life is not worth living.
They will be back soon. Finish, finish.
Your life is unexamined. Your life is unexamined.
Your life is unexamined. Your life is unexamined.
Stop.

(She thinks and regroups—walks downstage to mic.)

Okay. I eat muffins for breakfast. Almost every day. I've tried to switch to other things, but I love them too much. Blueberry is my favorite. I savor the way the blueberries feel in my mouth, before they burst. I have one cup of good coffee in the morning, a cappuccino or a café con leche. A very big cup. I try and eat light for lunch, like a salad or a yogurt. If I don't watch what I eat, I will blow up like a balloon, and yes, it has been harder after having the kids. I sometimes take an antianxiety medication. I was always kind of against it. But then I started yelling at the kids a lot. I would catch myself yelling when there really wasn't any reason to yell like,

I don't know, telling them to brush their teeth. And then I tried one of my friend's pills and I found it to be very comforting and helpful. And I didn't yell. So I asked my doctor for a prescription.

I have this fear that I am becoming one of the zombies. People on the meds seem to have an abnormal lack of passion, but I guess that's why they don't yell. I'm sure you know what I mean.

IOWA OF MY MIND

Barbara Cassidy

CHARACTER: SAMANTHA, a woman mid- to late thirties

PLACE: A bare stage

CIRCUMSTANCE: Speaking to the audience.

SAMANTHA: I used to have this idea about thinking and doing. It went like this.

If you thought something or had the desire for something in thought, you might as well do it because the thought is practically the same as the action. Now that seems a little crazy, especially if you're talking about someone getting hurt. But is the morality of the person the same if they mentally desire something, is it the same as if they did the thing? The idea came from a probably very immature idea of love, which basically was if you really truly loved someone, you would not be attracted to anyone else at all. I mean, you might be attracted in a very superficial way, but not in any real connected love way. You might say, "He's cute," etc. etc. but you will have no real desire for that other person. So that if one did have those thoughts and desires for another person and if that one was in a relationship with me, well, I would have said, "Go, go off with that other person, because if you're thinking about it, you might as well do it." I was in no way interested in being in a relationship with someone who was pining away for someone else, but not pursuing it out of some obligation or sense of loyalty to me. That just seemed so pathetic. Actually, it still does, in some ways. I still think I would rather my lover sleep with another but be totally in love with me. This I would prefer to him sleeping with me and being in love with another. The mind interests me more than action. Commitment of the mind, feeling . . . matters in some ways more than the actual doing of something. The doing is somewhat of an afterthought.

But now my mental conundrum is, if thinking is so important, then what kind of person does that make the person who's thinking "bad" things? This I wonder. Can they still be "good" people if they think bad things?

OUT OF FOCUS

Geralyn Cassidy

CHARACTER: HAPPY, an actress

PLACE: A bare stage

CIRCUMSTANCE: Speaking to the audience.

HAPPY: My most frequent roles are diner patron and pedestrian, not sure what that means. But I want to read to you some examples of casting notices for less typical background roles that I get online. If you can fit yourself into a category that is less populated, you are cutting your competition. It might be a special skill you have like juggling or even having a police uniform in your closet that gets you work. And who doesn't have a police uniform in their closet. I am now competing with Wall Street bankers as well as attorneys for background work. It seems many actors want to be lawyers and lawyers want to be actors. So I will read this list of casting notices to see if you might fit into any role. So the first listing is for *Actors Available with a Workable Dog*. Does anybody know what this dog does? Does he work the fields? Here's one, *Parents to Portray Trick-or-Treaters*. *Send a picture of yourself in your costume*. Now of course this notice comes out nowhere near Halloween. It is assumed you have a lineup of costumes in your closet. So this next listing is for *SAG Members with Interesting Mouths: Gold Teeth, Crooked Teeth, Unique Lips, and Braces*. Some of us straightened our teeth in hopes of obtaining work. Then a few days later, they simplified the notice so it read: *SAG Members with*

Missing Teeth. Hipsters are constantly sought. If you have to ask what a hipster is, you are probably not one. Here they are looking for a *Hipster with a Fixed Wheel or Fixed Gear Bicycle*. Now a fixed wheel or a fixed gear bicycle is a bicycle that has no free wheel, meaning it cannot coast down a hill, that thing you did as a child. Sounds like a lot of work. Here's one: *People Who Have Been Trained to Stand Posed*. I didn't know there was training for this. Maybe you can include playing statue as a child in that training. How about *Clowns That Do Evil*. I thought all clowns did evil after Stephen King's *It*. You don't hear many parents telling their kids to go play with the clown. Here's one with a personal connection: *SAG-AFTRA with Nun's Wardrobe*. Okay, my aunt was a nun . . . their wardrobe was not so extensive. They might have been better staying with habits. But by the look of my closet lately, I may have to apply. Now the next one also has some meaning to me as it involves a casting notice for the program *Blue Bloods*. My mom is a big fan of *Blue Bloods*. She loves that Wahlberg guy. Anyway, the show is looking for *Actors with Cocktail Attire*. They want cocktail attire and if you have ever seen the show, it's no surprise. The cocktails are on a constant flow there. But besides having cocktail attire, it says: *Must Be Comfortable with Rats on the Set*. Just what you want at a cocktail party, some rats. This last one is for: *People with Diseases*. In this case you *Must Have Hepatitis C*. And it is not enough that person has this disease, but it says they also *Must Be in Reasonable Shape, Kickboxing Is Helpful*. So there you go. Time to move on.

OUT OF FOCUS

Geralyn Cassidy

CHARACTER: HAPPY, an actress

PLACE: A bare stage

CIRCUMSTANCE: Speaking to the audience about her recent experience on a TV set.

(PRODUCTION ASSISTANT 1 [*Directing* HAPPY *on set*]: *Anyway, when you come in, okay, you're already in . . . but when you come in, do not pay attention to the two main characters who are having a slight altercation. Just sit down, eat your pie. Very important, we just had a pie-eating contest, that you eat the pie, talk without talking, and the director has asked that you show that fringe. That is part of the reason you were hired. Show the fringe.*)

HAPPY (*To audience*): Okay, so there is a man being gagged and bound at the door to this café and my reaction was an eye roll.

(*Tilts head slightly, rolls eyes.*) That's all. So I don't quite understand all this. He wants me to sit down, talk without talking—I love that one—and eat my pie as they had a pie-eating contest. What kind of contest is this? How much pie does he expect me to eat? Who would want to be in such a contest, let alone win it? Oh, yes, I just won the trophy for eating the most pie. Let's celebrate by going out to dinner.

Um . . . it looks like they're having a problem with the lights, so I'm going to tell you a few little tips that keep me going, just in case you want to do this kind of work. So the first thing when you get on set, do not look at the main actors. Don't stare at them. Don't even glance at them. They are from another world and I don't mean the soap opera. If you find yourself glancing at them, pretend you are looking at a clock above their head. Another thing is don't take out your iPhone and pretend to be talking to someone and snapping pictures instead. It doesn't work. They'll confiscate that phone. Also, be alert when you do these jobs. And I say this because there is an actress, I think her name is Dana Delany. She was on one of those very (*Sarcastic.*) uncommon CSI-type shows. So Ms. Delany said that a lot of the people, the background, that play dead bodies, and we know there is a lot of work in television for dead bodies, the background are being replaced by stunt people. Stunt people who ride motorcycles risking their lives are now going to get the background work for dead bodies. And the reason she said this is happening is because the dead bodies were falling asleep on the job . . . (*Pause.*) and snoring. She also said that some of the dead bodies were complaining a bit because some of them were being poked and prodded too much. And if you've ever watched the show, Ms. Delany does a little too much poking, if you ask me.

But anyway . . . and the last this . . . and I want to make sure . . . (*Looks stage right.*) Okay, they are still working on the lights . . . (*Turns head back center.*) When you have friends and family and you want them to see your work—maybe watch it yourself first, because you may not be in it as much as you think. For example, my mom . . . I'll say, "Mom, I am in something, but it's background work. I don't know how much I will be in it." She'll say, "Oh, I know, sweetie, but I want to see it." So she sits down (*Grabs a chair and sits.*) like she's going to watch an epic, she thinks she is watching *Gone With the Wind*, she gets a comforter, she gets a bowl of popcorn and puts it on her lap . . . and I start it and I enter and I exit *(**Pantomimes, grabbing a bowl of popcorn, puts kernel to mouth**.)*—before she can eat any popcorn. And she stares blankly at the screen and says, "That's it?"

So that's my advice.

THE DEMON HUNTER
Nat Cassidy

CHARACTER: ROBYN, a Latino single mother, in her thirties

PLACE: A psychologist's office

CIRCUMSTANCE: Speaking with Sam, her therapist, about her ten-year-old son Max, who has been committed to a hospital's psychological ward for observation.

(**SAM:** *So, tell me, what happened with Max?*)

ROBYN: He started seeing more and more. I mean "seeing," he began thinking he was seeing more and more. Getting in trouble at school. Getting in trouble wherever we went, screaming things, curses, "I know you!"

And at home, he would wander around the house, muttering. Lighting fires. I found him in the bathroom one night, middle of the night, he was naked and he'd built a little, uh, like, teepee under the sink, he said it was an altar, and he'd lit it on fire. That's when I kinda stopped sleeping.

It didn't get violent until about six, seven months ago.

(**SAM:** *Is that how you got that bandage on your hand?*)

ROBYN: Huh? Oh, ha—no, no. I got bit by a parakeet, if you can believe it.

(SAM: *A parakeet?*)

ROBYN: Yeah. I'd just visited Max for my daily, y'know . . . And I actually stopped by the mall to try to, I don't know, feel normal. And there was a display by the pet shop. Bird just flew at me, it was nuts.

(SAM: *Wow.*)

ROBYN: Yeah. Happens. Nothing new, since I was a kid, me and animals.

(SAM: *You were saying about violence . . .*)

ROBYN: Right. Little things at first, fights in school, then he got suspended for bringing a weapon.

(SAM: *A weapon.*)

ROBYN: A knife from our kitchen. Waving it around with his skinny little arms. We got kicked out of our supermarket.

And then finally I brought a man home. Like, on a date.

(SAM: *Do you date much?*)

ROBYN: What do you think? But, you know, I guess I thought he's not a baby anymore, I should be able to have a life, right?

(SAM: *Of course.*)

ROBYN: I'd been seeing this guy off and on for a little while at that point. But I'd stopped feeling like I could go out, because of how things were. And he kept asking, so I caved, I invited him over, not to spend the night, but just to have dinner, pretend I was an adult with needs and working parts and . . .

(SAM: *It didn't go well?***)**

ROBYN: Max wouldn't stop staring at him. I mean, unblinking.

And then he went back to his room for the rest of the night. The whole night, couldn't get him to come out. Which kind of dampened things. But the guy and I tried again, a couple more times actually. Over a few months. You know, it was clicking. Like, maybe I could have a boyfriend for the first time in . . .

(SAM: *That must have felt great.***)**

ROBYN: Yeah.

So we decided to try to go out to dinner one night to a restaurant. This is a big deal for me. I don't make a lot of money, I don't meet a lot of men, I've got maybe two, three more times in my life where this is gonna happen, right?

You can probably see where this is going. At the restaurant, about thirty minutes in, Max literally jumps on the table and tries to stab him with a steak knife. Shrieking the whole time, "I know what you are, I know what you are." Over and over again. He actually got the knife in. Not far.

The guy decided to press charges. But the court was willing to let it slide if Max underwent a psych eval. Enter Doctor Ericson.

ROW AFTER ROW

Jessica Dickey

CHARACTER: LEAH, a Civil War reenactor

PLACE: An old pub in Gettysburg, Pennsylvania

CIRCUMSTANCE: Speaking with Tom and Cal, other Civil War reenactors; the question just raised was "Can you imagine actually stabbing someone with a bayonet?"

LEAH: Definitely.

(CAL *and* **TOM** *look at* **LEAH.)**

(CAL: *You can.)*

LEAH: Yeah.

(CAL: *A bayonet into another man's body . . . ? You could do that . . . ?)*

LEAH: Yes. I could do that.

(CAL: *No way.)*

(LEAH: *Why do you say that?)*

(CAL: *No way.)*

(LEAH: *Why not?)*

(CAL: *Because that's just not natural. There is nothing natural about shoving a bayonet into another man's body.*)

LEAH: When your life is in danger? You'd be surprised.

(CAL: *Well, sure, thousands of soldiers did it. I'm just saying there's nothing natural about it. I mean, not like any of us here would actually know about this because we live in 2011 and we don't really have to fight for our lives on a regular basis or anything.*)

LEAH: I have fought for my life.

(CAL: *No, I don't mean like metaphorical, Joseph Campbell kind of shit—*)

LEAH: Neither do I. I have literally fought for my life.

(TOM: *Really?*)

(LEAH: *Yes.*)

(CAL: *Like really . . .*)

(LEAH: *Yes, Cal.*)

(TOM: *What happened?*)

LEAH: A guy attacked me on the subway.

(TOM: *Someone attacked you?*)

LEAH: Yeah. A year ago. I was riding home from a late-night catering job, just a money thing I was doing, and he was the only other person on the train with me. He was sitting across from me, like I was here and he was about where that chair is—and at some point he came over to where I was sitting, pretending to look at the map, like here, and he said, "Excuse me, do you know which stop is next?" And I said one forty-fifth—and the next thing I knew he was shoving himself on me, like grabbing all over me—and I couldn't breathe, I'm not sure if he had his hands on my throat, or—and he smelled like grapefruit and diesel fuel—And at first I was sort of paralyzed, like I wasn't sure if he fell over 'cuz the train jerked or something, but then when I couldn't breathe and I felt him, I felt him squeezing my breast hard, like *really* hard, there was this moment that I understood I was being attacked.

(TOM: *Holy shit.*)

LEAH: And I started screaming—or honestly, it was more like roaring, like a mythical *pig lion* or something; I fucking kicked and screamed with all my might.

(TOM: *Jesus Christ.*)

LEAH: And I think I surprised him or something because he almost immediately backed off, or maybe I actually kicked him off or something—and then he tried to run away, like to the other end of the train, like to here (*She moves the chairs.*) and I just *roared* at him—and then right then the doors opened and he ran out and that was it.

(CAL: *Jesus Christ.*)

(*They sit stunned for a moment.*)

(TOM: *And that was a year ago?*)

LEAH: Yeah. And I went to the hospital and got checked out and was basically just badly bruised. Like the next day my legs and arms were all bruised everywhere. And then, like, a month went by, and I realized that something just wasn't right. And it got very, very dark in my life. It's been very, very dark for what feels like a long time. And here I am.

SISTER CITIES

Colette Freedman

CHARACTER: CAROLINA, forty, uber thin, A+ personality, lawyer, recently divorced

PLACE: Their mother's modest living room in Poughkeepsie, NY

CIRCUMSTANCE: Carolina has just rushed back to her childhood home in Poughkeepsie, NY, with her younger sister Baltimore. Their other sister Austin is already there.

CAROLINA: Wait. Wait. Wait. Mom's in the bathroom? Our mother's in the bathroom?

(*Rushes into the other room.*)

(*Silence.*)

(BALTIMORE: *She looks good.*)

(AUSTIN: *I thought so.*)

(*They continue to eat in silence.*)

(BALTIMORE: *How've you been?*)

(AUSTIN: *I've been better.*)

CAROLINA (*Rushes back. She is furious.*): Mom's in the tub.

(BALTIMORE: *That's what I said.*)

(AUSTIN: *That's what she said.*)

CAROLINA (*Looks at her sisters as if they're crazy. Goes to the phone. Dials. Into phone.*): Can I have the number for the—(*To her sisters.*) Who do I call?

(BALTIMORE: *Nine-one-one?*)

(AUSTIN: *The coroner?*)

CAROLINA (*Into phone.*): Hi. Yes. May I please have the number for the police. **(***To* **AUSTIN.)** You are completely inept. (*Into phone.*) Hello, my mother's passed away and I'm not sure who I should talk to about . . . What? Okay. (*To sisters.*) She's transferring me. I thought you could at least take care of this before I got here.

(AUSTIN: *And miss this drama?*)

CAROLINA (*Into phone.*): Hi . . . Yes. Who do I talk to about getting a body removed? . . . 730 North Diversey Avenue . . . two blocks west of Greenspring . . . What? Uh, no, technically, it's not, I mean, I grew up in it, but I don't live here now . . . it's my mother's house, *was* my mother's house, but it *is* my mother's body . . . What? No, I found her dead . . . She slit her wrists . . . Because her wrists are slit. Yesterday . . . Because I wasn't here yesterday. I was in Seattle, litigating a case . . . Yes, I flew. I took the red-eye. American flight number twenty-two. Obnoxious stewardess—

(AUSTIN: *Flight attendant.*)

CAROLINA (*Glares at* **AUSTIN.** *Irritated.*): They showed a Leonardo DiCaprio movie, but I'm not a Leonardo DiCaprio fan, so I didn't watch it. Enough details? Can we please focus on my mother's corpse rotting in the tub? . . . Thank you. (*To sisters.*) He's transferring me. Is everyone completely incapable?

(AUSTIN: *Government worker.*)

(BALTIMORE: *Bureaucracy at its best.*)

CAROLINA (*Into phone.*): Hello. Hello . . . Yes. My name is Carol Baxter-Shaw and my dead mother is in the bathtub. I need you to send someone to pick her up . . . Yesterday . . . Because I wasn't here. (*Growing irritation.*) . . . Because I was under the false impression that someone else *had* called yesterday. (*Looks at* AUSTIN.) Because she's mentally unbalanced. (*Losing it.*) CAN YOU PLEASE JUST SEND SOMEONE OVER HERE TO REMOVE THE FUCKING BODY?! (*Composing herself.*) Thank you . . . Two to three hours? . . . Yes, I'm certain busy metropolises like Poughkeepsie are littered with dead bodies you people need to pick up . . . 730 North Diversey Avenue . . . D as in David, I.V.E.R.S.E.Y. Thank you. (*Hangs up phone. To* AUSTIN.) Do you have anything to drink?

(AUSTIN: *It's noon.*)

CAROLINA: I didn't ask for the time, I asked for a drink.

SISTER CITIES

Colette Freedman

CHARACTER: MARY, an attractive woman in her sixties; former dancer

PLACE: Her modest living room in Poughkeepsie, NY

CIRCUMSTANCE: Mary is ill and can't walk. She speaks to her daughter.

MARY: Look, I've already come to terms with this, and I need you to understand. I'm taking control. It's not going to get better from here. I can try to fool myself or use my last few months to "find" myself, but I don't have to . . . I'm not lost. I've enjoyed the journey . . . and now, I'm ready for it to end. Help me, Austin.

(*No response.*)

MARY: Okay. Get me a spider from the garden.

(**AUSTIN:** *Why?*)

MARY: Get me a spider. There are plenty hanging around the tomatoes. Go on, I'll still be here when you get back, I'm not going anywhere.

(**AUSTIN** *exits.* **MARY** *talks to the audience.*)

MARY: What I miss the most is the sex. No one ever thinks about senior citizens having sex, but we do. And we like it. We like it a lot. It's . . . slower than it was when we were younger. But the hormones are still active. Even after my men dried up, I didn't. I guess that's why God created masturbation. I can't even move my fingers that well anymore . . . You can't imagine what it's like to be trapped in your own body. Maybe, if I were a couch potato my whole life, I would have been used to this sitting thing, but I was a dancer. I had . . . the most beautiful legs. I'd sometimes dance sixteen hours a day. My feet were bloody until I was twenty . . . And I used to complain . . . Imagine that. I used to complain that my feet hurt. It's funny the things you complain about which really don't seem that serious in retrospect. Once, I was on a cruise with husband number three, Dallas's father. That man loved the water. Wonderful cruise. Too much food. Crappy ports, but, overall, pretty wonderful. Quite luxurious. So the day comes when we return to the States and for some reason the crew hadn't anticipated that everyone would want to leave the ship at once, so the lines to get off went around the ship, twice. You've never seen people so angry. It was like the entire previous fifteen days were negated by the two hours of inconvenience these people had to experience. I even felt myself getting antsy, and I'm not that antsy of a person. With four daughters, how can you be? The guy behind me . . . tall, balding, with extremely kind eyes said, very quietly, "We could be waiting in a line for bread and water." Wow. Now, there's a perspective . . . I'm not angry anymore. I was. Boy, was I. When I started to feel the stiffness, I cursed my body for getting older. When I started to have trouble breathing I cursed the scientists for not finding a cure. When my body shut down around me, I cursed God for . . . just for. He's an easy target, you know. But He's also comforting. Someone who listens, unconditionally . . . I've had an amazing life. I saw the world. I had four successful daughters. And I don't want to die in a hospice with tubes down my throat. I don't want to wait in line for bread and water. I'm ready.

(AUSTIN: [*Enters with a small Tupperware container.*] *Mom?*)

MARY (*Looks at her, manages a smile.*): Are you afraid of spiders?

(AUSTIN: *What do you want, Mother?*)

MARY: I want you to do exactly what I say. No deviations, no per-mutations. Promise?

(AUSTIN *glares at her.*)

MARY: Don't make a dying woman beg.

(AUSTIN: *Fine. I promise.*)

MARY: Pull two legs off of the spider.

(AUSTIN: Ew.)

MARY: Just do it.

(AUSTIN *dumps the spider on the table and gingerly pulls off two legs, grimacing.*)

MARY: What's it doing?

(AUSTIN: *Nothing. It's not moving.* [*Stares at the spider.*])

MARY: That's because you've taken away its mobility. Now, that spider is completely alive and, if spiders can hear or think, she's listening to this. And she's trapped. She'll die because she has no one to feed her, unless you want to take that task upon yourself.

(*Beat.*)

If she could talk, she would beg you to end her life. What kind of existence is this for a spider? Her friends and family are in the garden. They were happy there. They could go wherever they wanted. Eat whatever they pleased. Now, she's trapped. She can't move. She's going to die. The question is, how long will she have to live in pain before she's put out of her misery?

(*Beat.*)

What are you going to do, Austin? She's waiting.

(*Suddenly,* **AUSTIN** *smashes the spider with a book. She starts crying and looks up at* **MARY.**)

MARY: I'm ready to go, darling. Please, let me go.

SISTER CITIES

Colette Freedman

CHARACTER: DALLAS, thirties, attractive, perpetual sorority sister. Teacher, uptight, married. The "perfect child."

PLACE: Her mother's modest living room in Poughkeepsie, NY

CIRCUMSTANCE: Her mother has just died. Dallas and her three other sisters have gathered to make arrangements. It is the first time in years that all four girls have been together in their childhood home.

DALLAS: Children are supposed to leave the nest. That's the theory of evolution.

(*Beat.*)

I had an abortion.

(*Beat.*)

I was going to tell you. But this didn't seem like the right weekend to bring it up. Ya know, cause we're having so much fun.

Two weeks ago. I had an abortion two weeks ago. Still think I can't handle the ugliness of life in my perfectly pristine world?

I thought I wanted kids. We do. We did. He does. But I don't. I always thought I'd have kids. Lots of them. I guess I had painted this life for myself and it was going right on track . . . Marrying my college sweetheart. Building up a nest egg, but then . . .

I guess I realized that I'm really happy with the picture I painted. I don't want to frame it. I don't want to be Mom. I know I'm supposed to want them, but I don't. At the end of the day, I want to jump into my sweats and pour myself a big glass of red wine and watch bad reality TV. I want to be selfish. I want to have sex with my husband and take vacations and sleep through the night. I don't want a baby. I don't want kids. It wasn't until I got pregnant that I realized it.

(*Beat.*)

I didn't tell Peter. I couldn't. I told him I was going for my yearly pap smear and I did it, right in the office. I made him dinner that night. I taught the next day. Life goes on, right?

SISTER CITIES

Colette Freedman

CHARACTER: AUSTIN, thirty-six, athletic, gay. A successful writer. The second of four girls, Austin was the sister who lived with her mother and took care of her.

PLACE: Her mother's modest living room in Pough-keepsie, NY

CIRCUMSTANCE: Austin's mother, Mary, has just died. Her three other sisters have gathered to make arrangements. It is the first time in years that all four girls have been together in their childhood home.

AUSTIN: I can't write. I write one fucking book, which manages to land on the *Times* bestseller list and all of a sudden, I'm a fucking celebrity. People expect things from me. I can't figure out my own life and other people, strangers, expect things from me. I'm completely paralyzed. I've been frozen and I can't melt. I don't know how to. I have no idea how I wrote that book. I just did it. It came out.

(*Beat.*)

Do you know how many self-help books I own? I've tried every-thing: Yoga, meditation . . . even Kabbalah . . . but I didn't get the whole red string thing. I mean, if you're gonna find yourself, shouldn't you do it privately . . . not announce to the whole world,

"Look at me" . . . I have a red string . . . I'm Madonna. I'm not Madonna.

(Beat.)

Madonna was the perfect mother, right? Not, "Like a Virgin" Madonna, the "Is a virgin" Madonna—the Virgin mother. The Virgin Mary. Ha. Our Mary was no virgin. She slept with the fucking gardener. So the original Mary has Jesus, who becomes God, right? So then our Mary has Austin, who she decides to make God. To whom she generously bestows the power of life or death.

(Beat.)

But I have to give her credit. She asked for help. She wasn't afraid to show her weakness. I'm terrified. What happens when people realize I am far less than they expected?

(Beat.)

After the success of my book and the money and relationships that came with it, I realized that no one knows who I am. They pretend to. Hell, they read a book and they suddenly think they know me. But they don't know me. Mom didn't know me. She raised the bar so fucking high, so impossibly out of reach. I could never live up to her expectations.

(Beat.)

Fuck. My instincts are shot.

SISTER CITIES

Colette Freedman

CHARACTER: BALTIMORE, twenty-six, a free-spirited bohemian. Harvard grad student. The "baby of the family."

PLACE: Her mother's modest living room in Poughkeepsie, NY

CIRCUMSTANCE: Baltimore's mother has just died. She and her older three sisters have gathered to make arrangements. It is the first time in years that all four girls have been together in their childhood home.

BALTIMORE (*To* AUSTIN, *the sister who lived with Mom.*): Who died and left you boss?

(*Beat.*)

Oh, I guess Mom did.

(*Beat.*)

This is so fucked up. You know that? I mean, I was around.

I had vacation time. I wanted to come home, every break I had, but no . . . You guys were always saying travel, stay at school, study. How much do you think there really is to study when you're majoring in sociology?

(She grabs a Russian doll off the shelf and opens it, pulling out the dolls inside one by one, setting them down.)

You know the problem with these fucking dolls? The smallest one has absolutely no purpose. See, you've got this big one. The one that holds all the other ones. And you realize that she has a purpose. She's the mother. She contains all these other dolls inside of her. Protecting them. She's like a kangaroo, and all of these other dolls are like baby kangaroos safely tucked away in her pouch. So you've got the mother. Then the big one who everyone revered. The talented one who everyone worshipped. The perfect one who everyone admired.

(She has opened four of the dolls, revealing the tiniest doll. She holds up the "baby.")

And then you get to the end and there's this tiny doll, this shitty little piece of wood . . . with absolutely no purpose. The baby. She doesn't hold anything inside of her. Hell, you can barely see her. I call her . . . Baltimore.

(To **AUSTIN**.*)* You didn't let me say goodbye.

E-MAIL: 9/12

Midge Guerrara

CHARACTER: SERGEANT ALLY M. FORTE, an in-your-face female police officer

PLACE: A bare stage

CIRCUMSTANCE: To audience; taken from a real email the day following the events of 9/11.

ALLY: Dropped Eleanor at preschool—just like a stay-at-home mom—not the guilty NYPD sergeant juggling stints at forensics with kid hugs. Yesterday—the start of my ever-so-sacred vacation. I dropped the kid at school and was killing time in the supermarket. My cop antennae zapped up when I hear the lady in Customer Service doing all this drama—

(*Note:* **ALLY** *can also imitate these other roles.*)

(**SUPERMARKET CLERK:** *A plane ran right into the World Trade Center—right into the World Trade Center!*)

ALLY: and I am thinking this lady is insane. It just didn't seem realistic. A friend comes into the market and he says—

(**ALLY'S FRIEND:** *Ally, did you hear—a plane hit the World Trade Center.*)

ALLY: I yanked my kid out of preschool, raced to my brother's and turned on the TV. Then the second plane hit. When it hit and the building was going down—I could actually feel the people in that building. No—really—I know it is strange—but I could freakin' feel the people. They started putting the call on TV that all police officers return to duty. I was on vacation and in the NYPD that means they—can—not—touch you. I could have gone out to play in the park with my daughter. But—I was watching the carnage and something kept pulling me—

Next thing I know—I'm driving my daughter to my aunt's in the Bronx. The radio is on—I need information. The pull to go and my need to know was so strong—I don't get that my four-year-old is absorbing this shit as well. I put on my uniform—my kid was asleep—I left. I don't get four blocks when my aunt called and puts my hysterical Eleanor on the phone. She woke up seconds after I left—like she knew I was leaving—

(ELEANOR: *Don't go to the president's house. Bad men will burn it down. Come back, Mommy. Come home NOW.*)

ALLY: I got her calm. The pressure on me—out of this world— something outside of me pushed me to drive directly to the Towers. All the streets were blocked. My uniform greased the path and I was allowed to drive down. I'll never forget it—mountains—I mean mountains—of debris, metal twisted, snow of gray ash falling. I see everyone running around covered in masks and all this gear— I asked the EMS people if they had any more masks and they didn't. They were just these silly paper masks anyway. The force kept pulling me deeper and deeper to the site. I was zoned out— kind of just walking toward the center and up to my knees in water from the hoses. Fireman kept yelling—

(FIREMAN: *Get the hell out of here—this place is unstable.*)

ALLY: I came alive and realized I needed to get out of there and find the commanding officer to see what I could do. The C.O.— he gave me a group of ten guys to supervise. He said:

(COMMANDING OFFICER: *Figure out what to do with them.*)

ALLY: I know some from the Forty-Second Precinct and then there were young guys—just out of the academy. I tried talking to them. They had been there the whole time—frozen. They were coherent but the shock numbed them. After the first plane hit, they followed the Bronx emergency service unit down. The EMS—they told these guys to—

(EMS: *Stand fast!*)

ALLY: The emergency services guys rushed in. They went in and the—the building collapsed on them. While these ten guys were "standing fast," they watched the EMS guys get trapped in the collapse. They watched people flying out the windows and crashing on the overhang. They watched f'ing horror and did what they were told—they stood fast. We are trained not to get involved emotionally but this . . . We did what we had to do while the crap was flying down. It was the papers that kept falling that struck a nerve with me—that was someone's something. I was curious, but not curious enough to pick up a paper and look—it was too personal—horrible to read. I'm thinking what were they doing and how the world just stopped for them. Blizzard of white shit flies in our faces. We blocked off areas and the "asshole stand-around watchers" would come over and ask the same stupid-ass question:

(PERSON ON THE STREET: *So what do you think is in that stuff?*)

ALLY: I say "concrete"—we don't want to create panic—try pulverized people, asshole—I never got a mask for thirteen hours—

all this stuff is floating around. Nightfall came and everything was black. The most interesting part of the day was going to the ladies' room in the dark with a gun belt on.

There was a fancy hotel nearby that opened its doors and had all its chefs feeding us and giving us what we needed. People were nicer to people than I ever saw people being. But those cops standing by—man, they are damaged. How do you watch people fly out of windows—and hear the sounds—the loud crash when they land—and not be disturbed. A bomb squad officer told me:

(BOMB SQUAD OFFICER: *The difference between dying and surviving when hell came crashing down was if a guy ran right or left.*)

ALLY: Man, water was up to my knees and the dust was like sludge— by the end of the night you could peel my skin off. I was itching so badly. I got in my car—contaminated it and remembered—got out and took off my clothes—my shirt, hat—threw them out right there. This early a.m., my whole forensics office wanted to go downtown to help and brass wouldn't let us—here we have people trained and ready and we are told to sit in our offices. I'll sit for the next two weeks—sit with Eleanor, read kiddy books and take the rest of my vacation. The television is off. Peace.

E-MAIL: 9/12

Midge Guerrara

CHARACTER: MARILYN, a floozy, fun fifty-something New Yorker

PLACE: A bare stage

CIRCUMSTANCE: To audience; taken from a real email the day following the events of 9/11.

MARILYN: Hey, girlfriend, glad you're okay. We are too—sort of. This sucks. Yesterday was the day that really was going to be the first great day of the rest of my life. Wrong! It will be the day I remember and want to forget. I was standing in front of City Hall—George late as usual—we were going to get our marriage license yesterday. I looked up and saw the smoke and then out of the corner of my eye I saw the second plane hit, I SAW THE SECOND PLANE HIT.

People were running for cover but there was nowhere to go, pieces were flying everywhere. There were these two people I remember most—two people holding hands not standing in line to start a life together—two people holding hands and dying together. They jumped out of the Tower. They fuckin' just jumped. They weren't the only ones, there were dozens of people diving to death. Some floated clutching tablecloths or something—floated—until a gust of wind yanked the fabric—then nose dive. Splat.

(*Note:* MARILYN *could imitate the following roles.*)

(ACTOR: [*Whisper.*] *Street gossip said the first fireman to die got hit by a jumper.*)

MARILYN: Son of a bitch. Son of a bitch. I stood there and watched that shit. Glued—like to the bullshit TV or something. What is wrong with this country? Billions of bucks spent—CIA, FBI, freaking army—and no one knew what was happening. Wedding postponed. Sell your stock in Trojan—returning to a life of un-protected, rampant sex.

E-MAIL: 9/12

Midge Guerrara

CHARACTER: MIRIAM, a woman of indeterminate age; an old, gentle soul

PLACE: A bare stage

CIRCUMSTANCE: To audience; taken from a real email the day following the events of 9/11.

MIRIAM: Remember you'd grab your notebook and I my sketch-pad—life was about making art. Today—theater of cruelty. How did I morph from impassioned young artist to the building manager for WTC1—with a corner office yet—and a view of the Statue of Liberty—ironic.

I had just sat down at my desk on the eighty-eighth floor when the first plane hit four floors above me. The building swayed. I was thrown from my desk—got up, grabbed my purse, and ran to open doors. Groping my way down floor to floor to floor, using my universal key to open locked access doors. Encouraging people to exit—passing those that couldn't. I wasn't thinking—just doing—directing running fireman up the stairways. Twenty-one—that number sticks—I got to the twenty-first floor and fell. Smoke was everywhere—I thought if I just sat down the air would clear—someone prodded me from behind—she lifted me under my arms—like a small recalcitrant child—and urged me

(Note: MIRIAM *could say these other lines.)*

(ACTRESS: *down the steps one at a time—to the street.)*

MIRIAM: We stepped outside—the second plane hit. The crowd held me up—surging down the ash-filled street. I was a block away when the first tower collapsed—shielded by the corner of Roosevelt School. The guy behind me hadn't rounded the corner—he was tossed like a Ken doll tossed in the sea—rolling and flipping down the block by the tide of debris.

Theater of cruelty—no applause. Am I a hero for opening doors? People have been calling me a blessed hero. No. Today and forever I will be agonizing about the people I didn't save: firemen I directed upward, the dying and handicapped people I passed on the way down that I couldn't drag to safety . . . the voices that have left the chorus. My inadequacy to save everyone. Curtain—last act.

"Reach out. Find everyone. Hold on for dear life." You cannot be a human being unless you can hear those voices. Anyone who could perpetrate this act has turned a deaf ear to the human song. You are solid gold, keep listening.

Love and peace,

Miriam

OUR LADY OF KIBEHO

Katori Hall

CHARACTER: SISTER EVANGELIQUE, head nun of Kibeho College

PLACE: Kibeho College, an all-girl Catholic school in Kibeho, Rwanda. 1981–1982

CIRCUMSTANCE: In the middle of the night Sister Evangelique cannot sleep. She is walking the corridor with a candle in one hand and her rosary in another, trying to pray. She cannot. She begins to cry when Marie-Clare, a young twenty-one-year-old student, appears in the shadows of the corridor. She cannot sleep either. They try to comfort each other.

SISTER EVANGELIQUE: If only those silly girls knew the consequence of their actions. Bishop Gahamanyi wants to close down Kibeho College because of them.

(MARIE-CLARE: *No!*)

SISTER EVANGELIQUE: Yes! Yes, all because of their little stunts.

(MARIE-CLARE: *He cannot close the school just because of a few spoiled ground nuts. They cannot stop all of us from going to school. They cannot.*)

SISTER EVANGELIQUE (*But they are, Marie.*): Unless they stop, they will ruin the dreams of every young girl sleeping in that dormitory. And every mother's too. I have watched many young girls plucking potatoes from their field, fetching water from the well with many a baby on their back. I have seen many young girls start life with bright eyes only to have them swollen shut by the hand of a man. If only they knew that there was much more to life than being a man's wife. My mother carried me on her back. Never learned to read. Never learned much. Well, I promised myself that I would never be like my mother. Fetching water, sewing, babies . . .

(MARIE-CLARE: *That will not be me either.*)

SISTER EVANGELIQUE: No, Marie-Clare. Not you. That will not be your life. You are too feisty for that. A man would kill you with that mouth of yours. (*She pinches* **MARIE-CLARE** *on her cheek.*) You should go into the nunnery. You'd be a good nun.

(MARIE-CLARE: *Like you?*)

SISTER EVANGELIQUE: Like me.

(*They sit in silence drinking in the darkness.*)

Next time they want to play their little games. You burn them.

(*She smiles to herself.*)

That should awaken them from their spell.

(MARIE-CLARE: *Burn them?*)

SISTER EVANGELIQUE: Yes, you have my permission. Truth and morning become light with time.

(*She blows out the candle.*)

MARLY FLORINDA DESCENDS INTO HELL ONE STEP AT A TIME

Anne Hamilton

CHARACTER: MARLY FLORINDA, a woman running for president

PLACE: A convention hall

CIRCUMSTANCE: At a podium on a stage. She gets heckled at various times.

MARLY FLORINDA: I am a passionate believer in the right to life. A baby is a baby from conception. It has the right to flourish and grow.

What's that? How do I feel about gun control? That's not my topic.

Abortion is wrong. It's murder.

What? Is a school shooting murder? Of course it is, you idiot. **(To the guards.)** Get her out of here.

As president, I would make sure that *Roe v. Wade* is rolled back. That abortions are not performed in our states. Our children have the right to live.

We will grow our country like we grew the cotton that lined the fields of the South. We will prosper. Everyone has the right to life.

The babies will grow, with or without their mothers' consent. They will be born and go to school and take part in the American dream. Americans are not butchers and I will change the laws to make sure that every baby has a fighting chance at survival from inside the womb.

Yeah, what about when they go to school?

The schools are safe. The schools are safer with guns. If the teachers had guns, the school shooters wouldn't get away with murder.

(*A baby begins to cry in the audience. It gets louder and louder.*)

Health care?

Look—We get those babies born and I don't care about what happens after that.

Now. Number two—health care. (*The baby is crying loudly.*) Hey, excuse me. I don't like noise when I'm talking. Take it outside now. (*She points.*) Yes, you two. Out. Now. (*The baby's cries begin to fade.*) As I was saying, number two—health care. I will bring down Obamacare and downsize the government.

What? Do I think it's ironic that I insist on bringing babies to life and then also insist on denying them health care and then sending them to school where they'll be gunned down because gun laws are lax? No. Where is the irony? Life is life. You bring a life here whenever it comes because it is life. We are the best country in the world!

(*She interrupts the heckler.*) Yeah, it's called Obama CARE. It's Obama HATE. Obama hates babies. He hates babies in the womb. He doesn't want to see them born.

Obama kills babies. And that's wrong.

You'd have to be insane to not think that killing babies is wrong.

Babies. Babies.

I want a baby. I want a baby to raise. To take care of, to tell what to do, to move around.

I want. I need. A baby.

(*Pause.*)

Does anyone out there want to be a surrogate mother?

(*She points.*) Not you.

(*She keeps scanning the crowd for candidates.*) We're out of time. I won't answer questions. If you're interested in the job, email my office.

(*She begins to exit, taking one step down from the podium. She looks back.*) We create jobs. No matter what you say. (*She takes one more step down from the podium. Suddenly, she disappears as if she has fallen through a trap door.*)

OFEM

Anne Hamilton

CHARACTER: SALLY PARSONS, an organic Ovo-farmer

PLACE: The Heartland, USA

CIRCUMSTANCE: The start of the growing season. The present.

(Lights up on SALLY standing at a podium. There is ambient noise of many people in the room, shifting in their seats. There is a very excited atmosphere.)

SALLY: First of all, I want to thank you all for coming to the first meeting of the Ovo-Farmers Emerging Network. Today is an auspicious day. We will band together as farmers and distributors to grow and sell only female-centric fruits and vegetables. Hence: OFEM—Ovo-farmers, like the egg, but without eggs. We will not grow eggs. We are vegans.

(She stops and smiles. She has gotten ahead of herself.)

Let me back up. My co-founder and partner, Kate Meehan, and I decided to start this organization after looking at our plates one afternoon at lunch. And what did we see? Cucumbers, braised squash. Carrots. *(She almost gags.)* Italian eggplant. And what did we think?

"Why are we eating all of this phallocentric food?" Think of it, people, how many times does the Farmer Man's (*She indicates the name with her hands.*) penis have to be shoved in our face before we wake up? The time has come to take back the fields from the male farmer with his string beans and corn stalks and celery.

We started the OFEM movement to provide feminists and feminist sympathizers everywhere with a source of food that they can truly enjoy. That they can consume in small, ladylike bites, without feeling that the male-centric food industry is literally shoving its penis down our throats.

We will grow only—are you ready for this?—round, vaguely egg-shaped produce. Think of it, ladies and gentlemen—non-GMO, organic, pleasantly plump edibles. Cherries. Potatoes. Pumpkins. Bell peppers. And, of course, apples.

Apples will be the symbol of our movement as we take back the garden, take back the farmers markets, and overthrow the tyranny of the roadside fruit stand. We will offer gorgeous, plump tomatoes— heirloom tomatoes. Peaches in season. And garlic with its offending stem cut off, yeah, I'll enjoy that. (*She makes the movement of castrating the garlic.*) Roundish, delectable lettuces in all colors and textures, with all their lovely peaks and valleys.

Who knows the benefits of eating an OFEM diet? Maybe researchers in the future will discover less aggression in males and females investing in this way of life. And an increase in empathy. Neighbors will no longer be shouting at neighbors. Road rage will decrease. Speeding—well, that may become a thing of the past.

Sisters, Ovo-farming—mark my words—may become the new way of life for the masses. But it starts here. Take a stand with me.

Say no to sugar snap peas. And YES to gourds. No! To corn. And YES! To watermelon. Hell, no! To zucchini and YES! YES! YES! (*She says this with orgasmic glee.*) To edamame.

In conclusion, thank you for coming to this historic event. Please leave us your email so we can be in touch, and remember the life-giving quality of female-centric plants. It's ovum, the egg; OFEM, the new true, right, and good food movement; and Oh, Femme! How we need you! So let us all take back our vim and vigor.

Say hello to a new way of life.

Thank you very much!

(*Wild applause erupts from the audience. Lights down.*)

GOING UP

Penny Jackson

CHARACTER: SIMONE, once a private school teacher named Winton

PLACE: A hotel elevator

CIRCUMSTANCE: Simone finds herself stuck in an elevator with Jack, a homophobic and claustrophobic auto salesman. Simone explains how she was fired as a teacher at a conservative school.

SIMONE: Yes. And the headmaster was an old army sergeant— hated anyone he said wasn't a real man.

(SIMONE *walks out of the elevator.* **SIMONE** *is now* **WINSTON,** *the schoolteacher.)*

(Sounds of school bells ringing and students' voices.)

SIMONE/WINSTON: But, Headmaster Greeley, Walt Whitman is one of the most famous American poets of the day. He was also an extraordinary American patriot, nursing the Civil War wounded.

(Beat.)

Yes, the poem we read was a love poem. This wasn't the first love poem the boys have read. We just finished *Romeo and Juliet*, if you remember.

(Beat.)

Did Daniel's father say that?

(Beat.)

But Whitman's poem was a love poem for a boy. How could I lie about that? Daniel asked me if Whitman wrote the poem for his girlfriend and I answered boyfriend. I know they're in seventh grade but half of them have already watched hard-core porn on their iPads.

(Beat.)

No, that wasn't an appropriate thing to say.

(Beat. Suddenly angered.)

That's a lie. I did not touch Ryan Smith in any way that could be considered the way you are indicating. I actually just patted him on the back because he was choking on a piece of gum. Yes, I know gum is forbidden in the classroom, but I couldn't allow him to suffocate! Brian's just furious because he failed his English final and I caught him cheating too. He copied his entire paper about *Macbeth* from an essay on Wikipedia.

(Beat.)

Yes, I'm aware that Ryan's father is head of the fund-raising committee. And just donated a swimming pool.

(Beat.)

No, I cannot do that. Ryan failed.

(Beat.)

Yes, that is my final answer. I understand the consequences.

(*Beat.*)

May I at least have a reference?

SEE SOMETHING, SAY SOMETHING

Penny Jackson

CHARACTER: MARY, a plump middle-age Hispanic woman, working class but more sophisticated

PLACE: A park bench in lower Manhattan. It is 2002.

CIRCUMSTANCE: Mary is sitting chatting with Mohammad, a Sikh doctor in his thirties, whom she's just met on the subway.

MARY (*Pause.*): This is tough for me.

(MOHAMMAD: *Then you don't have to speak about it.*)

MARY: No. I should talk. That's what my own doctor said. I have a lot of trouble sleeping, you know, and in the middle of the night, I eat. That's why I gained so much weight this year.

(MOHAMMAD: *Doctors are used to not sleeping as well.*)

MARY: So I should speak to you. See, I used to work down there. By the Towers. I mean, actually in one of THE towers. The North Tower.

(MOHAMMAD: *I see.*)

MARY: That's why I had to change offices since my office no longer exists.

(MOHAMMAD: *Were you there, Mary?*)

MARY: Yeah, I was there. I was the secretary to a real estate firm on the ninety-ninth floor. Eating these donuts, well, it reminded me.

(MOHAMMAD: *Who?*)

MARY: You don't want to hear this.

(MOHAMMAD: *Please. I do.*)

MARY: Well, it's because of the donuts, the Dunkin Donuts, is why I didn't die. Sounds crazy, right?

(MOHAMMAD: *Interesting. Please. Go ahead.*)

MARY: That morning, 9/11, well, I was really pissed off at my boss. He had a really big meeting that day. Another law firm my boss was trying to impress. My boss was hoping there would be a lot of moola in this new deal.

(MOHAMMAD: *Moola?*)

MARY: Money. Lots of money. Anyway, Bernie, my boss, he wanted me to buy donuts for this meeting. So I brought in a box of glazed donuts from Dunkin Donuts like I do every morning. But Bernie took one look at the box and went ape shit.

(MOHAMMAD: *Ape shit! I know what that means. Like to go crazy.*)

(MARY: *Yeah, like Joey.*)

(MOHAMMAD: *So what was the problem?*)

MARY: For some reason this lawyer who Bernie was hoping to impress would only eat donuts with the holes. Munchkins. Like the little people in *The Wizard of Oz*. Do you know that movie? Judy Garland?

(MOHAMMAD: *Of course. Somewhere over the rainbow. So Munchkins are also donuts, yes?*)

MARY: Yes. This lawyer was convinced that Munchkins taste better. Or maybe he had a phobia about donuts with holes. I don't know. But Bernie started screaming at me and I started crying and he actually took my box of donuts and threw them in the trash. Just like that. If our office was on the ground floor, I swear he would have dumped them right out the window. Can you believe this? I mean, Bernie going ballistic here. I know he's under a lot of pressure but this is no excuse. And then he tells me that I have to go out again and get them a box of these new donuts, Munchkins, and this big-shot lawyer will be here in eight minutes, so I have to hustle my fat ass. He didn't say fat ass, but I could tell he was thinking that there was no way I could move that fast. But I did. So I rush out without my coat, which isn't a problem since it was a beautiful day, but I'm like waiting for the elevator forever since it's on the 102nd floor, and then the elevator finally comes and by the time I'm in the lobby I have like exactly four minutes left. And there's a Dunkin Donuts in the concourse lobby, but there's of course a line about ten feet long. You know that always happens. When you're in a rush, everyone else is too.

(MOHAMMAD: *Yes.*)

MARY: It's like everyone decided at exactly 9:28 that they needed donuts and coffee. So I remember there's another Dunkin Donuts on Liberty Street. If I cross the street and run, I should be able to make it. Hold on, I need to catch my breath here.

(MOHAMMAD: *Please, take your time.*)

MARY: So I cross the street and I'm running and sweating 'cause it's a warm day and I want to scream SCREW YOU, BERNIE. This is bullshit, excuse my language. And I finally make it to that Dunkin Donuts on Liberty Street and the line is not too bad and I order ten glazed Munchkins and ten strawberry frosted Munchkins and another ten cinnamon Munchkins. The girl looks half asleep when she gives me the box and change, and then I'm back outside racing down the block and I'm looking at the blue sky and out of the corner of my eye I see this plane flying kind of fast. But I really didn't notice it because I'm looking now at my wallet and I realized that stupid girl didn't give me the correct change. I handed her a twenty-dollar bill and she gave me back three dollars, as if I gave her a ten dollar bill instead. She owes me thirteen dollars and if I come back with the wrong change Bernie's going to kill me and I'm already in hot water because I'm late with his precious Munchkins.

(*Beat.*)

Am I going too fast here?

(MOHAMMAD: *No. Please continue.*)

MARY: So I stop there right in the middle of the sidewalk pissed as hell and turn around to return to that store and I'm thinking, wait, maybe I got the wrong donuts since I seem to suddenly remember that Bernie is allergic to cinnamon. And that's exactly when it hits. WHAM! The plane. The tower. My office. Bernie. Janet. Rachel. Mort. Ramon, the guy who cleans the office. Sara, Janet's little girl, who was at the office that morning since she was sick and Janet had no one to take care of her at home. Everyone who works there. On the 102nd floor. On all the floors. And everything . . .

(*Long pause.*)

Everything stops. Later, all I can think is this was the best thirteen dollars I ever lost in my life.

ST. FRANCIS

Miranda Jonte

CHARACTER: TESSA BARTLETT, thirty-four, veterinarian turned rescue worker

PLACE: At her veterinarian office

CIRCUMSTANCE: Tessa is on the phone trying to place a rescue dog with a good home for her nonprofit rescue organization, One Paw, Two Paw.

TESSA: Bob, hey, it's Tessa. I'm good, thanks, how are you? Listen, I heard you're looking for another dog. Yeah . . . I've got your dog. She's a great animal. She's two. She's spayed, she's housebroken—

(The question she doesn't want to be asked. Hedging.) Uh, we've had her two years. It is a long time, you're right. Well, she's not the prettiest of dogs, but you don't want a beauty queen, you want a dog who'll go on your runs with you. No, she's not a Staffie, she's a Dogo. People mix 'em up all the time. Oh, Dogos are great dogs, they're smart, loyal, great with kids—and she loves other dogs, so she and Peanut will be friends for life.

We call her Elsa Lanchester. Well, like I said, she's not gonna win any beauty contests, so people have been a little shy about taking her home. . . . She was—you know what a bait dog is? Bait dogs are used in dogfights—no, she . . . Yes! It's what it sounds like. Actually! Aggressive traits are deliberately bred OUT of Dogos, so she was just a sitting duck, poor thing. We found her, and we fixed her up, and the staff here loves her.

Well, her left eye, the left side of her face, is, it's just a slope, actually, but she's got full mobility, great guard dog, very protective of her people . . . right. Uh-huh. Bob, I promise you, you couldn't ask for a better pet.

Right. Got it. (*Can't help herself.*) It's just funny, you know. Just funny. I think it's funny. Because you married a woman with no tits and no chin. (*Hangs up.*)

ST. FRANCIS

Miranda Jonte

CHARACTER: TESSA BARTLETT, thirty-four, veterinarian turned rescue worker

PLACE: Before a town council meeting in Arcata, a coastal town of Humboldt County in Northern California

CIRCUMSTANCE: Tessa addresses the council members, appealing the Arcata Council decision to deny the right of sale to her nonprofit rescue organization, One Paw, Two Paw.

(**COUNCILMAN STACEY:** *Next is Tessa Bartlett, appealing the Arcata Council decision of March 1st to deny the right of sale to One Paw, Two Paw. Tessa, whenever you're ready.*)

TESSA: Doctor.

(**COUNCILWOMAN PORTER:** *Excuse me?*)

TESSA: I said "doctor." I am a doctor of veterinary medicine. I went to UC Davis, I was a specialist in emergency and critical care, and was head of surgery at twenty-nine. I then began what was my clearly ignominious retreat into the far less noble world of rescue work, it is the hardest thing I've ever done—it is so hard, it is, it is ugly, the things I see, the people I deal with—the Randy Warrens—who is the greatest example of a coast redneck this town has ever seen. Please address me as doctor. I will be a vet for the rest of my days in our great state of California, because it is an ineluctable need.

I offer spay and neuter services—a service I insist on providing to this city for free—I stay a vet so that when I get a phone call on a Sunday to please make a house call to put down a fourteen-year-old German shepherd who is blind and incontinent, and who is the love of her owner's life, Stu, I do it. I'm a doctor. I field offers to this day to run emergency rooms. I got a call from Burlington, Vermont, this morning, to head their teaching hospital. I know you wish I were there right now. But this is my home.

And right now I'm the only no-kill shelter in the county, and you—everyone here—you're going to have to go home and tell your kids why there's no more story time at One Paw, Two Paw. You're going to have to tell your kids AND your parents what happened to all those dogs they love to read to, and walk with. And then once you tell them the "what," you'll have to tell them the "why."

You don't know what to do with me. I got that—I get it—I'm loud, I'm not polite, but you don't need to know what to do with me. Just give me the place on Harkness—sell it to me—*I* know what to do.

Thank you to the council for your time and attention. I'm just going to end with this: The world is a dangerous place to live, not because of the people who are evil, but because of the people who don't do anything about it.

ST. FRANCIS

Miranda Jonte

CHARACTER: TESSA BARTLETT, thirty-four, veterinarian turned rescue worker

PLACE: Afternoon, outdoors. The backyard of Tessa's father's house in Northern California

CIRCUMSTANCE: Tessa enters and finds her father in the backyard working. There are shovels, potting soil, a cinder block, bricks, etc. on the ground.

TESSA: (*Offstage.*) Dad?

(*She enters and finds him, somewhere out in the audience. She attempts to get his attention.*)

Dad? Hey, Dad! Hey. (*Leans against fence.*) Hi. (*Surveys backyard.*) What is all this, what are you doing? A pond? You're building a pond? Digging—a koi pond. You want some help? (*Making conversation.*) I heard that Hank's hips are getting stiff. Julie told me. She said she gave him Rimadyl, and Julie's a great vet, but I brought you glucosamine.

I don't know if you heard, but I won my appeal, and the city is selling me the plot over on Harkness. It's a great place for us. The thing is, I've only been given a week to make the transition. Crazy, right? There's construction that has to be done. There are codes. Plus, we're at capacity, and the dogs keep coming. I'm the only no-kill shelter in the county; these dogs have nowhere else to go. If I could give them away, I would. But people want to pay $7,000 for a fucking overbred piece of—sorry. Language. I love that you rescued Hank. Hank is a great dog.

(*Her big pitch.*) The trust that Mom left—I'd like to access it—not all of it, just enough to make the sale and cut a check so we can begin making the facility battle-ready for the dogs. I've got the Aaron Bros. in town, who will do the labor for free if I pay for the materials. Which is amazing, but I've only got seven days to make this happen, and it would kill me to have to turn down their offer. Starbucks takes over next week—I need quick cash. So, I'm asking you if you'll grant me access. (*Corrects herself.*) Early access. Dad, I know. I know it says when I'm thirty-five, but this can't wait until November.

Even if I went back to work at the hospital, I wouldn't get my first check for a month. I opened a shelter so I could be the on-site vet and put that money elsewhere.

So. Business proposition. You lend me the money, and in November I'll repay you from the trust. We can write up a contract and have it notarized and everything—and with interest. I'm not money-focused—

Why won't you help me? I know things have been not good since Mom died. And lately people say you don't answer the phone or the door. What's going on? And don't tell me it's in my head. What did I do to you?

(*Realization.*) The ring. Mom's ring. This is about Mom's ring. No. No. Dad, when you gave me that ring, you said, if you ever get into a tight spot and have to sell it, that's OK. You gave me the papers it came with! (*Stops herself.*) You cannot be mad at me for this. I know it was an heirloom. I offered to let you keep that ring twice. And you said no both times. Do you think that was fun for me? Do you think I wanted to do it? I was sleeping on the floor at the shelter. I had to replace my surgical equipment.

(*Gathers herself.*) I didn't do it to upset you or to spite you—and I understand that you're angry. I'm sorry, Dad. (*Baffled.*) Dad? Dad? Walter?

Okay. See you around, Walter. (*Leaves, comes back.*) Am I not an heirloom?

THE RISE AND FALL OF A TEENAGE CYBER QUEEN

Lindsay Joy

CHARACTER: LYLA, fourteen but looks twenty. She is tarted out wearing a ton of makeup, fake lashes, bright pink wig.

PLACE: A teenage girl's bedroom, in transition; pinks, purples, and butterflies juxtaposed with a few band posters and junior's-style clothing strewn about everywhere.

CIRCUMSTANCE: Lyla is recording another YouTube video of herself.

(LYLA *twirls in front of her mirror once. She puts another tutu-style skirt on under the one she is already wearing. She puts all her weight into one hip and looks painfully bored. Satisfied, she opens a MacBook. She sets it on a dresser. She tilts her head. She starts recording.*)

LYLA: Okay. Listen up out there. You—my *new* viewers—have stumbled down the rabbit hole. And I ain't Alice. This is LeilaniLuv. I spell that L-U-V for anybody that's just figuring out who the hell I am. I'm your Pop Princess Philosopher Supreme. I'm the number one, numero uno stickam poster in the U-S of A. And I'm planning on staying that way. So, you little bitches better hit that trend button on the bottom of my screen. Press it! You know you want to.

I'm kicking it old-school today. I'm talking Kurt Cobain, kids. Feeling a little angst-y. This whole semester has been super-duper trying. Like—I thought last semester was bad but *this* one—

Three words. Gym. First period. Gym at eight in the morning. So fucking mean. Kill me. My locker is like East Jesus away from the gymnasium . . . and class is filled with every girl that has hated me since kindergarten. Just to get through it—I have to envision the emo cheerleaders from this super-old video. Yeah. Remember videos? I was like two when MTV was still playing videos.

(**LYLA** *queues up "Smells Like Teen Spirit" and gears up to perform. She is ready to sing along. She gets close to the cam and blows a kiss. Her T-shirt dips down over her bra. She dances a little more out of control.*)

Awww yeah! Hyper moment!

(**LYLA***'s movements become more crazy. She dissolves to giggles. She crosses to the computer.*)

That is a good one.

(*She sits on her bed. She grabs a teddy bear. She sighs.*)

Don't leave just yet. Stay with me.

I want you to know that I get it. We—you and me—we aren't the popular kids. Bring me your geeks, your nerds, your thick-rimmed glasses . . . I get it. I hate those fuckers just as much as you do.

(*A knock on the door.* **LYLA** *rushes to her closet.*)

Just a second!

(*She runs back to the laptop.*)

LeilaniLuv signing off. Trend me! Microphone drop!

(She shuts the computer. Another knock.)

Gimme a sec. I'm changing.

(She throws off her wig and tee. She scrambles into a big sweatshirt and sweatpants. Another knock.)

One more second.

(She throws open some books and quickly scrubs makeup off with a cleanser pad. She opens the door.)

LAST CALL

Kelly McAllister

CHARACTER: KRISTIN, thirties

PLACE: A bar

CIRCUMSTANCE: Kristin is intelligent but stifled, stuck in a loveless marriage of convenience that she is afraid to leave. She is in a bar, complaining to her friends about Jerry, an old boyfriend who keeps writing her love poems.

KRISTIN: Oh, shit. Those stupid poems. Have you read any of them? He's so tragic. It's almost funny. He writes me poem after poem about his love for me. His great, unrequited love. How the two weeks we dated in high school were the golden days of his life. How he thinks of no one but me, even when he's with someone else. That's not love. He doesn't love me. He doesn't even know me. Not really.

(VINCE: *Jerry's just a . . . a hopeless romantic.***)**

KRISTIN: Keats was a romantic. Shelley was a romantic. Jerry is a prude.

I'll tell you a little secret. I took him to this special beach I like to go to in Carmel one night about a year ago. Just for fun. I asked him, since he's such the poet, if he believed in free love; he was shocked. He said that it wouldn't be right. That I was a married woman. Which is just so much bullshit. He doesn't love me. He just mopes, and writes poem after poem about how sad his life is. One thing I'll say for Karl. He never writes poems. **(*She takes her drink, sips it.*)** He's stable. No surprises. Ever.

(*She takes another sip.*) If I ever wrote a poem, I'd call it "Life Sucks—Get Over It." **(*She drains the rest of her drink.*)** Actually, I write poems all the time. Dreary epics about staring into the abyss, lost princesses stranded in distant lands. **(*Laughs.*)** Of course, I can't stand any of them. Stupid, huh?

(*To bartender.*) Another cosmo. **(*Music starts.*)** Wanna dance?

MUSE OF FIRE

Kelly McAllister

CHARACTER: **JESSIE**, early twenties

PLACE: In front of the green room in a college theater

CIRCUMSTANCE: Theater major Jessie has just found out that she has yet again been cast in a small role while her boyfriend, Mick, and rival, Emily, get the leads. Again.

JESSIE (*To* MICK.): You take it easy, asshole! You got cast in the lead. Again. Opposite Emily. Again. And I got the little supporting role. Again. And that stupid role is the biggest role this fucked-ass department has seen fit to give me in my four years here. Okay? Everybody get that?

In four years at this place, Celia is the biggest part I've ever gotten! I am a loser! Yeah, I'm fucking pissed, and there's nothing any of you can do to make me feel better. So just fuck off, and I'll be fine. Isn't this how we learn? By continually getting shat on? I must be a genius by now!

(*To* **EMILY.**) A good part? What do you know about a good part? I think it's great that you'll be Rosalind. Really, I do. You'll be great. But please don't fucking tell me how good my part is or I will seriously lose it.

SOME UNFORTUNATE HOUR

Kelly McAllister

CHARACTER: JANUS, thirties. A bartender.

PLACE: A bar in Denver, Colorado

CIRCUMSTANCE: Janus has carried a torch for Tom for a very long time, and finally lets her feelings out to him.

JANUS: I love you, you stupid son of a bitch! Okay? Get it? You're it. I know it. What did you say about love just then? I care about you more than anything in the world, idiot. In the entire fucking world. Me. Anything. Including—especially me. I worship you. I don't know why. You're a fucking asshole. But I do. I hate it, but I absolutely adore you. We're meant for each other, you stupid motherfucker. Open your goddamned eyes!

Who listens to your crazy shit? Who takes care of you? Who was there when the shit hit the fan and your so-called friends couldn't be bothered? Me, you colossal asshole! I'm good for you. God-damn it, I'm great for you, and you fucking know it! You know I am.

I'm hope. I'm your only fucking hope, you fucking moron! Grow a pair, you fucking Mary! Oh my God! Goddamn you! You parade your stupid shit, your bullshit little boy bullshit, in front of my face like I'm not there. Do I like her line? Do I like her fucking line?!? Fuck you! Fuck you twice and stick it in your ass. You're hurting me. I hurt. We were good that time. We were—how can we have had that and not be—You cried on my stomach! You cried on my stomach and I knew. I knew it. I'm—I'm home. I'm your home. Let me be your home. I love you.

BREEDERS

Bob Ost

CHARACTER: RITA JAMESON, sixties. Painter of large canvasses of flowers—honest and endearing. Careful in her speech, accurate in her observations.

PLACE: A gay artists' colony on the beach

CIRCUMSTANCE: Rita tells Joanne, also gay, of her past experience of having a daughter and secretly being a "breeder" (heterosexual).

(JOANNE: *Have you loved many men?*)

RITA: Made love to many. Been in love with . . . probably just one.

(JOANNE: *What was he like?*)

RITA: Young and handsome, like every man who is loved. We took art class together. He was so terribly shy, I think I probably spoke to him first—how forward of me, but if the truth be known, I rather enjoyed pursuing him. Finally I got him to ask me out on a genuine evening date. It took three dates before he tried to kiss me good night, or I should say, before he asked if he could kiss me good night. Of course, if he hadn't asked, I had every intention of suggesting it. It wasn't much of a kiss, really—just a timid little peck on the cheek, but that's when I first thought I might love him. I did decide then and there that he was going to sleep with me.

(JOANNE: *Didn't you like women?*)

RITA: I suppose I'd always had an attraction to the comforting softness of the female form—it was what I preferred painting even then, though I never suspected that my interest might be more than artistic. But I was telling you about the seduction of my young artist. It took four months to maneuver an invitation to his room—he lived at school, and literally had to sneak me into the building.

(JOANNE: *What was it like?*)

(RITA: *What was what like?*)

(JOANNE: *Being made love to for the first time.*)

RITA: I'm afraid I didn't find out that night. I managed to get him in bed with me all right, much to his apparent surprise—though Lord only knows what he thought we were going to be doing in his room. But after we'd been lying together for a few minutes, and the things that I thought should be happening somehow weren't, I noticed that he was crying—just a few tears shining in his sad, brown eyes, and he look at me ever so hopelessly, and apologized. He didn't have to tell me he was homosexual, because I knew it right then, and felt as if I'd known it all along.

THE FORTIFICATION OF MISS GRACE WREN

Robin Rice

CHARACTER: GRACE, an elementary school teacher in New York City

PLACE: A park bench in front of a statue of Peter Stuyvesant. East Village, New York City, a few weeks after the tragedy of 9/11.

CIRCUMSTANCE: Grace has been traumatized by 9/11 and has been afraid to go back to school and face the questions her students will ask about the tragedy. She is gaining strength from talking to a statue of Peter Stuyvesant, the first governor of NYC, in the park.

GRACE (*To the statue.*): Sarah Leibowitz in the last row by the windows, cried out, "What are those birds, Miss Wren? What are those funny-looking birds—holding hands—not flying, falling?"

Those are people, Sarah. I didn't say that. My tongue froze in my mouth.

There was a body on a bedroom floor, blown through the glass. I didn't see it. Someone told me. I couldn't listen. There was a man sitting on a bench covered with ash. I couldn't look.

Walking here this morning, I couldn't see past my feet on the bloody sidewalk. I was too afraid to raise my eyes. Too afraid to let anything in. Afraid even to see strangers taking the hands of strangers. New Yorkers, guarding their breath with masks as they posted photographs, lit candles, said prayers. New Yorkers, leaning out of windows to applaud heavy equipment arriving from distant states, rolling into town, headed downtown. Trucks crowded with workers on their way downtown. Heroes going to empty streets downtown.

You tell me to stand strong, to fight back. Fight? My city is wounded enough. Enough tears. Enough blood. You don't need eyes to know that. Bring on the sirens. Bombard me with pictures that won't go away, but I will not tolerate more violence. Know this, though: I will not stand silently if anyone anywhere threatens to touch a hair on the head of one person—one statue—one child in my city ever again. I'm fighting back my own way.

I see myself standing behind my desk, beneath the flag, black towers of smoke rising outside, thirty-two young faces looking to me for answers.

I won't turn away from them again.

QUEEN FOR A DAY

Robin Rice

CHARACTER: LILA, thirties, crippled and homebound

PLACE: Her modest home

CIRCUMSTANCE: Lila depends entirely on her twelve-year-old son. When he wants to visit a new friend, it throws her into a panic.

LILA: Don't go. What about my show? What about the garage window? What about your jacket zipper? What about—what about the clock?! What about the fireplace damper? What about the—the washing machine spinner? The—the porch swing. Everything! Everything's broken or breaking.

Oh, Arnie, at night I feel the rain. I feel icicles stabbing under the edges of the roof. They're melting inside. They're soaking the house. It's going to tear apart like paper. Maybe tonight. Maybe this afternoon. The house is tearing apart. I'll freeze. The radiator in my bedroom is cold. You're supposed to bleed it. My father would tell you that. It was always: Bleed the radiators! Bleed the radiators! Like you'd be saved if only you'd bleed the friggin' radiators. I don't know how to do it, but I know I should.

Never mind. It won't make any difference. The furnace is broken. I'm going to freeze to death. Maybe it's not broken. The light is out in the basement. I don't know. I can't tell. It's dark.

The flashlight corroded. The candles are lost. Okay, I hid them. I don't want you lighting candles all over the house. Please, honey! You'll burn yourself. You'll blow up the house. Stop, Arnie! It's a big goddamn *furnace* and you're a twelve-year-old boy. You can't fix a furnace from a home handyman book.

Besides, I . . . I called the repairman. You have to stay until he gets here. A couple of hours. Maybe. You know how they are. Maybe he won't show up. Repairmen aren't dependable like you. I depend on you.

When he comes, if he comes—can you stay then too? I'm afraid to have a repairman in the house when I'm alone.

MALA HIERBA

Tanya Saracho

CHARACTER: FABIOLA, twenty-five-year-old daughter of a wealthy border magnate. Latino.

PLACE: Her father and stepmother Liliana's master bedroom in their home in Texas

CIRCUMSTANCE: Liliana is trying to nap when Fabiola enters the room in a freaking tornado of tears and *Housewives of the Rio Grande Valley* drama-rama. Yuya, the family maid who raised Liliana, is in the room.

FABIOLA: . . . Aaaggrr . . . he's a fucking asshole! Mydad'sa motherfuckingasshole! Oh my God! I can't stand him! I can't fucking stand him. I want him to fucking fall off a cliff.

(*Some crying. It's deep for* **FABIOLA** *right now.*)

I'm like completely . . . He's totally cut me off!

(*She holds out five credit cards. Gold, platinum . . . BLACK.*)

He canceled them all! My Saks card, my Macy's card. He cancelled . . . HE CANCELED MY NORDSTROM'S CARD FOR FUCK'S SAKE. What am I going to have to shop at fucking Old Navy now?!

(*Slight breakdown.*)

My gas card. He canceled my motherfucking gas card! You know what that means, right? That I can't fucking go anywhere. That means I'm trapped here.

(YUYA [*To herself.*]: *Ay no, Dios mio.*)

FABIOLA: What the fuck am I supposed to do with my mother-fucking life right now?!

(LILIANA: *What happened? Your dad's in Guadalajara. He's not even . . . calm down, Fabi. Calmadita . . . when did you talk to him? Is he here?*)

FABIOLA: Yeah, on the phone just now. And now he hung up on me and won't answer.

(LILIANA: *Fabi, is he here?*)

FABIOLA: I want to kill myself right now.

(LILIANA: *Fabi, what happened?*)

FABIOLA: He saw that I wasn't going to school.

(LILIANA: *He what?*)

FABIOLA: I haven't . . . I'm not in school right now. I just needed some time to figure some stuff out. . . . Hey, I don't need the righteous shit right now, okay? I don't need judgment right now, Liliana.

(LILIANA: *You haven't been going to school?*)

FABIOLA: No. But that's only because I didn't enroll, okay? And the thing he doesn't see is that I made that decision with like a clear adult mind. It wasn't like my first two years where I had to drop out of classes because I wasn't going, you know? Because I overslept or because, well, most of my professors were total douche bags. They didn't know what the hell they were talking about. Whatever. That's not even the . . . But why can't he see that this time, I made a conscious, responsible decision. To actually not waste money and time and whatever aggravation. I consciously didn't enroll this semester. Alright, I didn't enroll this whole year. Okay? I didn't enroll this year and well . . . He got all—Oh God, he scared the fuck out of me. He was like King Kong. You know how he gets like King Kong.

(LILIANA: *Yes.***)**

FABIOLA: Yeah, but he never gets like that with me.

(LILIANA: *I know.***)**

FABIOLA: And he just . . . took it all away. He's never done that, Liliana. I'm like really scared right now because he's never done that. Even when I went to rehab for the . . . I mean he was like more caring than he was mad. Oh my God, I'm going to kill myself. That's what I'm going to tell him. That I'm going to kill myself. See how he'd like his only daughter to . . .

(LILIANA: *Shh. Calm down, calm down, Fabi.***)**

FABIOLA: Don't fucking tell me to calm down! Are you listening to me?!

ELEPHANT

Margie Stokley

CHARACTER: ELLEN, twenties, an artist

PLACE: Her studio

CIRCUMSTANCE: Newly pregnant, she is speaking with her boyfriend, Jay.

ELLEN: You're a romantic.

(JAY: *You hate me because I'm a romantic?***)**

ELLEN: No. Yes! You buy me CDs, get me flowers, and a dog. A dog you now doubt I will remember? Even though he is living and breathing in the same house with me?

(JAY: *I didn't mean it like that.***)**

ELLEN: Jay. You said, "Be aware he is here." (*A pause.*) You said . . .

(JAY: *I know.***)**

ELLEN: I am carrying . . . you can't even trust me with a dog. How can you trust with a child? (*A pause.*) Jay, Look at me . . . I'm a mom. Do you see a mom?! Because I am not like your mom. She is a mom! I am fat, emotional, selfish, and, for the past few weeks, mean. I can't smile. It's really hard for me to smile. I thought love would fuel me . . . not suck me dry. I am perpetually in shock. Ever since—you entered my studio . . . you . . . you! Soft, sweet, smiling you . . . and every time you leave . . . I think, good! Go! I could use some time alone. But then you go . . . and you are just gone and I wish you were here.

(*He hugs her.*)

ELLEN: I'm pregnant and we live in Jersey.

(JAY: *I know.*)

ELLEN: I was nicer when we lived in Arizona.

(JAY: *No. No, you weren't.*)

ELLEN: Jay, stop it. Don't make me laugh. Nothing is funny.

(JAY: *Okay. [Jay begins jumping up and down.] Marry me.*)

ELLEN: I'm pregnant and we aren't even married . . . don't say it . . . I know what you are gonna say . . .

(JAY: . . . *you wanted to wait.*)

ELLEN: Well, congrats! You win. I lose. I'd only known you for two weeks . . . two weeks! I didn't want to ruin it.

(JAY: *Let's ruin it and get married now. Marry me.*)

ELLEN: No. (*A beat.*) Of course. I'm having a child and my life is over . . . over! We met and you have been great ever since. You are great! Your whole family is great. I am not great. I don't know what I am. I suck.

PRETTY THEFT

Adam Szymkowicz

CHARACTER: SUZY, eighteen. Suzy has been previously arrested for vandalism and had an abortion.

PLACE: A pharmacy

CIRCUMSTANCE: Suzy is shopping in the Health and Beauty Aid section with her friend Allegra. Allegra is saying that she had wanted to be Suzy's friend in the sixth grade.

SUZY (*Putting other items in her bag.*): Well, I wouldn't shut up, would I? When you don't shut up, the boys notice you. Course, eventually you realize no one was really listening. And you stop speaking up in class—realize maybe you weren't saying anything anyway—not something someone else couldn't say better—usually a boy. And the boys who seemed to be listening to you weren't quite the right boys.

(ALLEGRA: *Sometimes I wanted to hit you.*)

SUZY (*Stuffing her pockets.*): So you stopped talking. But then you realize if you lift up your shirt there are boys that like that too. But maybe those aren't quite the right boys either because then later those boys want to see what's in your pants. And want to put themselves in you even if you're not ready and maybe those aren't the right boys either but at least they need you for a few minutes.

(ALLEGRA: *And you wore those skirts.***)**

SUZY (*Stuffing her bag.*): Then you go after your friend's boyfriend because it's wrong and it's fun and because your friend is pretty. And you get him but once you have him, you realize he's no good. And your friend hates you. But you do it again anyway to another friend. And all the girls all begin to hate you. They call you a skank and they call you a whore. But some of the boys like you some of the time. But they think you're a slut. So you embrace it because what else can you do? You buy a T-shirt that says "Fuckdoll" and a series of short skirts and you try on provocative lipsticks.

PRETTY THEFT

Adam Szymkowicz

CHARACTER: ALLEGRA, eighteen

PLACE: A hospital room

CIRCUMSTANCE: Allegra is talking to her father, who faces away from us. He wears an oxygen mask and does not move. He is unconscious.

ALLEGRA: And I'm working at this like group home with Suzy Harris. We hang out a lot. You know who she is? I think you'd like her. She's a lot of fun. She was supposed to come here with me today but . . . she couldn't make it.

Bobby's good. He works at the garden place in Salem sometimes on the weekends. He wishes he could be here too. He's, uh . . . a good boyfriend. I think it'll last for us. One of the great . . . things.

Fuck! It's just as hard to talk to you now that you can't talk back. I can't ever say the right thing to you. You're just so . . . not there, aren't you. You always ignore me. I know even if you can hear me right now, you're not paying attention. You never . . . Why don't I matter to you? What do you want from me?!! Maybe you just want to be left alone.

Well, that's what I'll do then. I'm sorry I disturbed your death bed, you selfish fucking bastard! You self-centered, egotistical, pompous fucking bastard! I don't care what you want! I hope you die! I hope you fucking die real soon! You can fucking rot and be eaten by worms! I hope fucking worms eat you! Worms with big fucking teeth! And rats and flies and vultures! I hope vultures dig you up and take you out of the casket and fly away with you! You fuck!

(*Pause.*)

I miss you.

I've always missed you. I'm sorry. I don't want you to die. I'm sorry. I'm sorry. Oh, Christ, I'm so sorry. Please don't die. You're so small. Please, Daddy.

(ALLEGRA *kisses his forehead.*)

PRETTY THEFT

Adam Szymkowicz

CHARACTER: ALLEGRA, eighteen

PLACE: Allegra's house, immediately following her dad's funeral

CIRCUMSTANCE: Allegra's mom sits, facing away from us, watching TV. Allegra did not attend her father's funeral.

(ALLEGRA *approaches her mother.***)**

ALLEGRA: I know you're probably mad at me for leaving before the funeral, but I just can't do it. My whole body itches and it won't stop until I get in a car and can't see this house or this town or this state from the rearview window.

This way is better. This way I'll come back from my trip and go straight to school and you won't have to look at me or think about me. You can tell people you have a daughter but you won't have to talk to me on the phone or see me on the couch. I'll be a no-maintenance daughter just like you always wanted.

I'm going to go now. I know someday you'll want to talk to me again. Maybe after I graduate and get a job and get married and buy a house and have my own daughter. Then you can talk to her and be her favorite and then we can pretend you were a really great mother. She won't know and I don't have to tell her. But now I'm going to get on the road and push you out of my mind and I probably won't think of you until I get to the Grand Canyon or some other fairly good canyon and maybe I'll cry in front of the mammoth orange hole in the ground or maybe I'll smile because it's so beautiful and I'm free and windswept.

But first I'm going to get into Suzy's mom's car and we'll drive till there's just drops left in the tank and as we cross the border into Massachusetts, we'll roll into the first gas station where I'll get some Ding Dongs and some orange soda and I'll bite into the first one sitting on the hood, watching the car slurp up gas. Then I'll get in the driver's seat and put my foot on the accelerator until I can't keep my eyes open anymore. So I pull over and we both close our eyes and sleep until we're awoken at 3 a.m. by separate but equally terrible nightmares.

RARE BIRDS

Adam Szymkowicz

CHARACTER: JANET WILLS, mid- to late thirties. Single mom to Evan, sixteen.

PLACE: Outside the door to Evan's bedroom in Colchester, CT, outside Hartford

CIRCUMSTANCE: Janet has been having trouble with Evan, and has been warned that he may be trying to hurt himself. When she tries to open his bedroom door to speak with him, she finds it locked. He refuses to open it. She's been there for a while. What she doesn't know is that Evan is inside his room with a handgun.

(JANET *is slumped, sitting on the floor in the hallway, leaning against his bedroom door. She has a drink. It's definitely alcoholic. Gin and tonic? Bourbon? She clinks the ice cubes in her glass. Takes a drink.*)

JANET: I'm still here. I'm not going away.

(**EVAN:** *Go away.*)

JANET: Let me in.

(**EVAN:** . . .)

JANET: I take partial credit for all this, okay? It's my fault too.

(EVAN: *Good.*)

JANET: You want to tell me why your principal is calling?

(EVAN: *No.*)

JANET: I feel like I don't know you anymore. I used to know you. We used to hang out all the time. People told me. They said it would be like this to have a teenager. But they also said you would come home drunk. I guess you're figuring things out, right?

(EVAN: *Stop talking.*)

JANET: I will not. You will open the door. Are you opening the door?

(EVAN: *No.*)

JANET: I'm trying. I really am. You know that, right?

(EVAN: *Yeah.*)

JANET: It's not easy. I'm not saying I thought it would be easy. I don't know. I could use some help. It's been the two of us and that has worked sort of but also it's not working at all. If only your father was here. The way he had with people. He was amazing, wasn't he, in his interactions. He would know how to talk to you. He made people feel good about themselves. It didn't matter if he was talking to a mechanic or a doctor. Everyone liked him. That's who he was. I don't know who he was.

Do you remember his funeral? The whole town came. They said it was the biggest turnout they ever had. For weeks people came by with dinners they made, cakes, breads. But then, eventually, they stopped coming and they forgot about me. It was him they liked, not me. I was just a reminder he was gone. And now I go into the grocery store and there's no recognition in anyone's eyes. Maybe they don't want to remember him. Or maybe they were never really his friends anyway. I don't know. Or maybe too much time has passed. Or maybe they found out. Some of them must have known. In a small town like this—You don't remember, do you? I hope you don't remember. I tried to keep it away from you. What he did. And how he did it. I thought I knew him. And then with one quick action he made it clear I didn't know him at all.

I don't know why he left us. He was just lost. I could see it sometimes in the way he looked off in the distance. He wasn't there, wouldn't let me see. So charismatic all the time and then moments where he wasn't there. The darkness. Still. I never thought—Which is why it scares me so much that you're having such trouble. A man like him could do that, then you with all the problems you're having. Evan? Evan, baby?

Evan? Evan, honey, are you there? Evan? Can you let me in?

(EVAN: *No.*)

JANET: Should I be worried? Is this something to worry about? (*Pause.*) Evan?

(EVAN: *Go away.*)

JANET: I'm going to break the door down. I'll get the sledgehammer. I'll get the axe. I'll knock it down.

(*Beat.*)

Evan—You're not like him, are you?

WHEN JANUARY FEELS LIKE SUMMER

Cori Thomas

CHARACTER: NIRMALA, Indian and born in India, young, pretty

PLACE: A hospital room

CIRCUMSTANCE: She sits next to her husband's bed; he is unconscious on a ventilator. Ishan is Nirmala's brother.

NIRMALA: I've told Ishan that I hate you but I don't hate you. If you hear me, Prasad, I don't hate you. But I hate what you have done to me. You took a young girl from India, and you promised her parents you would be a good husband, but you weren't. How you made me feel. A handsome man like you. And everyone thought you wanted me to be your wife because you thought I was beautiful and suitable. Because my family was low compared to yours, how could I say something. What would my mother think of the real reason I have no children? The doctor says you're not improving. But I can't kill you. I've thought about why I wait. I'm waiting to understand why I wear a bindi and call you my husband, and work at your shop, and cook and clean even though you never . . . On our wedding night, I waited for you. I heard you snore and I knew you were asleep. And I thought it was the days of fun and dancing. And we left India the next day, so then I thought it was the time difference, that perhaps you were tired from the traveling. Every night, I waited for you to turn towards me and enjoy me. And when I used to look at you, I thought . . . I'm lucky. My eyes were very pleased by what I saw, Prasad. And I could imagine you touching my cheek, or touching my arms, or my legs, and my back, and my neck, and my skin. And I wished you would. Every minute I wished you would, even just once. One night I turned to your back and I put my arm around you and I felt your body pull away from me, and I felt you hold your breath, and I could almost hear you saying, "don't, don't, don't . . . touch me." And so I turned back to my own side. I took my arm from around you and I turned away to my own side.

(*Beat.*)

After they shot you, I put those magazines and tapes in a box and I closed it. And I wrote the word trash on it. I put away your days and weeks and nights and months and minutes of unclothed women who don't look like me at all. Those aren't even real people that you know, Prasad. I'm sure you never knew those people. But you preferred them to me. And now people have seen that box. Ishan has seen it. Joe has seen it, I know he has. And now they know you did not find me pleasing. How can you still be hurting me from there? Well, now, these days, if I want, I can lift your arm and put your hand close to my skin, and make you touch me. And you can't move away. Here is my chance at last to feel your skin next to mine. But it's not the same, is it? What good will it do? But I can't let these people unplug this machine. Even though I have a good reason, I can't do it. Every morning I wake and I wash my face, and I brush my teeth, and I comb my hair, and I place the bindi to my forehead and I remember what it means to wear one. It means that I'm your wife, Prasad, whether or not you liked it. It means that I'm your wife until you die.

ARRANGEMENTS

Ken Weitzman

CHARACTER: DONNA, early forties. Obese. Sexy, smart, fierce, and funny. Often a bull in a china shop, though her destruction is always calculated.

PLACE: A flower shop

CIRCUMSTANCE: With Ros, Donna's younger sister, mid-to-late thirties, at her flower shop. Ros is obsessively body-conscious for fear of becoming Donna.

(ROS: *What about, what about a job? Don't you have a job down there?*)

DONNA: Jenny Craig Fitness. I was fired.

(*From* **ROS***'s reaction.*)

Not for my weight. It's actually part of their corporate strategy to have someone like me in the sales department. It's in the manual. A customer comes in, sits with me, and I tell them, "Of course *I* haven't done the program. Would I look like this if I did? No, I'm waiting for my one-year mark. You see, after an employee has worked here a year, they can do the program for free. See those women over there, the ones pretending to be on business calls? The ones who look like supermodels? They were just like me once. Then they did the program and now look at them."

I had the routine down. I signed a lot of customers. No, it wasn't the sales. It was the phones. All ringing at the same time, all day. All day. It made me, I'd look at the customer and feel compelled to tell the truth.

(ROS: *And what was that?*)

DONNA: That my supermodel coworkers were in grave danger. There was a phenomenon going on in Florida. It was hurricane season. And in strong winds, women like that were being swept up, blown away. People didn't realize it because they stay indoors and away from windows during storms. But if they just looked out the window they'd see it. Hundreds of skinny supermodel women flying through the air, being swept away by the wind.

It can be beautiful to watch.

(*Beat.*)

You used to find me amusing.

THE ASK

David Lee White

CHARACTER: SALLY, a woman of any age

PLACE: A restaurant

CIRCUMSTANCE: Out for dinner with Darren, a multi-millionaire, who thought Sally was asking him out on a date when in reality she was only planning to ask him for a big donation to her nonprofit theater.

(*Realizing his mistake and the awkward position he is in,* **DARREN** *gets up to leave the restaurant.*)

SALLY: Wait. (*Finishes her drink in one gulp.*) Okay. Let's do this.

(**DARREN:** *Do what?*)

SALLY: I'm lonely, you're lonely. I can do this. I mean, why not?

(**DARREN:** *I don't understand.*)

SALLY: I mean, just because I wasn't keyed into it doesn't mean there wasn't something between us. Looking back on it, I can see how you might have found me very attractive and how all the talking and getting to know one another and making jokes and the asking out and everything . . . I can see how you might have perceived that as a date situation.

(DARREN: *I did.*)

SALLY: So let's go.

(DARREN: *Go . . . where?*)

SALLY: I want this. I mean, maybe I want this. Actually, for sure, I am definitely, maybe ready for a relationship.

(DARREN: *Uh . . .*)

SALLY: I mean, we've got some differences to overcome, sure. We're from different worlds and all that. I'm a simple girl that lives within my means, you know? And you're an extra-special rich guy with golf clubs and snow-globe doorknobs and Monet paintings in the bathroom—

(DARREN: *I don't really collect art.*)

SALLY: But you gotta know something about me. Sometimes, I'm fucking crazy. Like really emotionally needy, like cry-for-no-reason crazy. But—BUT—it's only because I'm so full of passion!

(DARREN: *I can see that.*)

SALLY: And here's something you gotta know about me. I mean, if we're gonna be together, this is something you have to learn to embrace.

(DARREN: *Yes?*)

SALLY: I love art. Love it. Look at me in the fucking eyes and you'll be able to see how serious I am. Serious like cancer. Sorry. A heart attack. I love everything about art. And you know what the best art is? Theater. I love the way it makes me feel. I love the way it frees my mind. I love the way it breaks down the walls of convention and makes us ask questions that we never dared to ask. I love the messed-up red chairs that hurt my ass and the pretentious production photos in the lobby. I love the stupid sweatshirts and the overpriced Shakespeare paperbacks in the gift shop.

But most of all, I love the people that make theater. I love how they cuss in front of each other in the workplace like it's something to be proud of. I love how the actors flirt with each other and give one another unnecessary backrubs. I love how they can go from laughing to crying in about two seconds and mean absolutely every bit of it. I love how they eat nothing but couscous but still manage to smoke enough cigarettes to choke a pack mule. I love how they blame everyone else for the fact that they don't make enough money. I love how the directors scream and insult everyone they meet so they can sound smarter and more passionate than the rest of us. I love the theater technicians that absolutely refuse to do anything productive until they've bitched for it for at least an hour. I love that.

My God, I more than just love those people. I want to be those people. I want to live my life on the edge. I want to have sex that I only barely remember. I want to argue about politics and pretend that I watch the news. I want to complain that there's no cot in the dressing room. I want to be difficult and cranky and have bags under my eyes and a constant, small, hacking cough that spreads through the entire cast until it becomes pneumonia.

So are you ready, Darren? Are you ready to take that leap with me? Are you ready to be on the fucked-up roller coaster for the rest of your life?

MEN'S MONOLOGUES

AFTER

Glenn Alterman

CHARACTER: TOM, thirties or forties, attractive, sensitive

PLACE: A café

CIRCUMSTANCE: Talking to another friend.

TOM: There was a steam room at our gym where Hank and I worked out. Wasn't very well lit, this steam room, and was always filled with, well, steam. Was right after he had helped me, spotted me with some weights.

After I finished my set I said something like, "Thanks, appreciate it." He smiled and I left, went to the locker room, changed, and went to the steam room. Then, a little later, we sort of bumped into each other in the steam room. We accidentally brushed up against each other. Told you it wasn't very well lit in there. And we both stood there, just . . . Didn't move, didn't say anything. Just looked at each other and . . . Then, almost at the same time, we touched. Just . . . touched each other. My hand on his shoulder, his hand on my chest. We stood there, touching, staring at each other. Didn't say anything. Was just silence, except for the sound of the steam. We touched some more, face, hips, everything. Slowly, gently. And that was it, that was all. We left, without saying a word.

But . . . well, eventually it became a regular thing. The steam room, we'd meet there and . . . I know this might sound crazy, but every time we met it was more *meaningful*. The touches, more caring, sensitive. Then kisses, caresses, embraces. Then holding, just holding each other. He . . . Hank was a very loving man. I know that sounds . . . Especially since we never really said anything except "Hi" and "Bye." But I knew it, could feel it; I *knew* him. And sure, sometimes we did have sex but the sex wasn't really important.

Anyway, it always seemed so strange to me how little I really knew about him; I mean about his life . . . I certainly didn't know he was married.

(*Softly, sadly.*)

I miss him, more than you can imagine. More than anyone I've ever known. After he died—I quit the gym.

NOBODY'S FLOOD

Glenn Alterman

CHARACTER: BARRY, mid-twenties to late thirties; very caring

PLACE: An apartment

CIRCUMSTANCE: Talking to his mother about the death of his brother.

BARRY: Reason I came here that night was that Mickey had called me, Ma. Said he needed me. We'd been speaking on the phone for months. A lot of talks. Anyway, I came over that night to try and talk him out of it. We argued, I yelled. But you know Mickey. He just wanted one thing—to go down to the ocean with me. Said he was too weak to get there by himself, that he needed my help. I kept saying no, I wouldn't. But finally I agreed. He told me it'd become like a war zone with you too, and he was the battlefield. How everything was getting too crazy. How he couldn't take it anymore. And you know how he loved the water, the beach. Was gonna be his one last hurrah. He threatened to crawl down there if he had to. And so finally, as usual, I gave in. I . . . I just wanted him to have some dignity. I mean if he was gonna do it . . .

So I carried him down to the beach. We sat there, had like a little party. Was crazy. We talked about old times, growing up, even told a few jokes. But then he got like real quiet. And we just sat there, in the dark, listening to the ocean. He drank some more vodka, took the pills. I just watched. I didn't know . . . Then he hugged me, said, "I love you, Bar." Told him I loved him too, always would.

Then he stood up, and, I don't know how, but slowly walked down to the water. I got up, followed him down there, still hoping he'd change his mind. Then I watched him go in, swim out 'til . . . I couldn't see him anymore. Till he just like disappeared. I just stood there at the water for a while, watching the waves come in. Still hoping . . . Then . . . I left, went to the airport, waited for Brenda.

WITH A BULLET
(OR, SURPRISE ME)

John Patrick Bray

CHARACTER: DONNY, thirties

PLACE: A diner

CIRCUMSTANCE: Donny is talking to Pidge about his affair with a friend's estranged wife. Donny's own wife and autistic son were shot dead in a robbery. Donny discusses why it was easier to sleep with a friend than to try to date again.

DONNY: I stopped at Tantillo's for gas. About a month ago. And I saw her there. Little J in the back. We start talking. I tell her that I like Tantillo's. It's friendly. Familiar. Best buttered hard rolls in the valley. Don't know what they do to those rolls. So. I buy her one and Little J one. We talk for a while. You know, Gina didn't know Archie had autism? Big J never told her. He doesn't believe in things like that. Thinks it has to do with label-happy liberals. Bad parenting. I don't know.

So, I tell her about how when we'd ask Archie where he was going if he left a room, he'd say, "to get answers." Or if we asked him how he was feeling, he'd say, "looks like rain." Even when we were inside, he'd say, "looks like rain." It took me two years to figure out that he did that because he liked the control. If you say "looks like rain," folks invariably look up. They can't help it.

And I'm thinking these things and saying these things to Gina, looking at Little J, who's sitting on my trunk looking bored. Archie never looked bored, so it's new to me. And we keep talking. And I'm eating this hard roll, and for the first time in a while, I'm not thinking about . . . but what I am thinking about is Little J and Gina. Being on their own. About me being on my own. So, the next night, I take Gina out. We hit the diner on the other side of town, I know Big J likes the one that's on this side. And we've done that three times. Came here last week.

(*Beat.*)

So, yeah. It's good. She knows what happened. I don't have to talk about it. A friend of mine had wanted to set me up, you know? On a date? But, with a blind date, I'd have to talk about it. With Gina? There's nothing to talk about.

LINER NOTES

John Patrick Bray

CHARACTER: GEORGE, late forties, early fifties. Former lead guitarist for the rock-and-roll legend Jake Sampson. Now an adjunct math professor in South Carolina.

PLACE: Jake Sampson's grave

CIRCUMSTANCE: George visits Jake's grave for the first time, with Jake's twenty–year-old daughter, Alice. George is in the process of divorce from his longtime wife; in this scene we discover that George has always loved Alice's mother.

GEORGE (*To* ALICE.): So, what the hell did I come here for?! Jesus, I risked a lot to—

(ALICE: *I didn't see any tabloids hanging around your apartment.***)**

GEORGE: Of course you didn't! What, you think the risk is Kathleen? Forget her, she's done. It's over there. And you know why? She left me. For my. BEST. FRIEND. A FUCKING colleague! Not my doing, nothing to do with writing a song for a girl once or twice, but because she fell in love with someone else. And I have to prance around like I'm Mr. Innocent—no past, no anything, just so I have a fucking leg to stand on in court.

(ALICE: *But she said—***)**

GEORGE: Right, "another one." You ever hear of "projection?" There was NO. ONE. Don't you get it?! I'M FORGOTTEN! Okay? I'm forgotten, Alice! Completely fucking forgotten. A big fucking plate-glass wall, with no one looking in. Jesus. Being next to Jake brings it all back, how fucking forgotten and fucking meaningless I am. I couldn't compete with that. The man had EVERYTHING, fucking EVERYTHING. He made sure of that. You read the Liner Notes! Those damn stories, the ego, the . . . the . . . do you even know the names of the other two members of our band?! He wouldn't leave anything for the rest of us.

(ALICE: *And HE felt forgotten, too, okay?!)*

GEORGE: And he had no right to feel that way. He won! He won fucking everything! He even took . . . which . . . you don't know what that was like!

(ALICE: *Well, you're the one who married Kathleen in a hurry!)*

(GEORGE: *Of course I did.)*

GEORGE: I'm not proud of why I married *her*, but God almighty, I just thought it would help me forget.

(ALICE: *You gave up on her!)*

GEORGE: I DID NOT GIVE UP ON HER! I tried, and it didn't work. I even tried to stay as a friend, but you know, being her married and having a kid—

(ALICE: *So, it is my fault.)*

(GEORGE: *I didn't mean—)*

(ALICE: *You make it sound like I was just something to keep you away.*)

GEORGE: Of course not. It was more complicated than that.

(ALICE: *What, you and Mom put on some Marvin Gaye and . . . you sleep with my mother when she was with Jake? [Beat.] Did you? [Longer beat.] Oh. Was I . . . was I around yet?*)

(Pause.)

GEORGE: You were around. You were . . . an infant. Okay? (*Beat.*) Things had . . . come to a head with Kathleen. I thought it was time to patch things up with your dad. So, I show up, unannounced. Your mom comes to the door, looking tired. Jake's on one of his binges. No idea where he was, when he's coming home. You were sleeping upstairs. You had a fever, so she kept checking up on you. So, I end up hanging out a bit. We start talking about, you know, stuff . . . and we fall asleep on the couch. Jake comes in the next morning, half drunk, half hungover. He sees us . . . and says nothing. He even makes us breakfast. Worst oatmeal of my life. We eat in silence. As I start to leave, your dad says, "This ain't the old days. Why don't you go home to your wife?" That was it. I took a long look at . . . at . . . she looks so tired, but . . . we had fallen in love again. And so . . . I went home. (*Beat.*) What do you want with me, Alice? Really?

LINER NOTES

John Patrick Bray

CHARACTER: GEORGE, late forties–early fifties. A former lead guitarist to the legendary rock-and-roll artist Jake Sampson, now an adjunct math professor in South Carolina.

PLACE: Jake Sampson's grave

CIRCUMSTANCE: George needs to make peace with his former friend, and speaks to Jake's headstone.

(GEORGE *looks at the grave, and slowly kneels on top of it, his arms around the headstone.***)**

GEORGE: Hey, Jake. You in there? Maybe your ego is, and that's the part I want to say this to. (***Struggles. Can't find the words.***) It was all for Jake, by Jake. Where the fuck was I in the equation, huh? You think, what, I wanted this life? *Why didn't I keep going?* I don't know. *Why didn't I have a band after you?* I don't know. You did your thing, and I just . . . I just . . . Kathleen was there . . . and I . . . I forgot who I was. I wanted to FORGET who I was. Everything. Because maybe if I forgot everything, I wouldn't feel like I had nothing. And so . . . here you are. And here I am. Fuck. (***Pause.***)

(*He reaches inside his jacket and places the picture of them together on top of the headstone.***)**

It's not your fault. It's not. I kept my lapel down, you know? I didn't . . . I kept going to school. I over-rehearsed. I geared myself for . . . for failure. Long before we stopped playing together. I mean, I worked so hard on plan B, that plan A just . . . poof.

(He holds Jake's headstone, like a brother.)

It's not your fault. I fucking hate you, but it's not your fault. None of it. Let that be in the liner notes. Shit. Your last two albums didn't have any. Maybe . . . maybe I can . . . I mean . . . maybe . . .

(Beat. He stands up. Looks where ALICE *exited.)*

I'll make it right, Jake. Son of a bitch. I'll make it right. *(Beat.)* Look at that. My shadow on your headstone.

NIGHTMARES: A DEMONSTRATION OF THE SUBLIME

Adam R. Burnett

CHARACTER: JUD

PLACE: A stage

CIRCUMSTANCE: Addressing the audience at the beginning of the play. An overture.

JUD: Here are some images from my trip last winter through the Southwest. We decided to take a little tour and we saw some wonderful sights and sounds—including naked vampires singing rock anthems at the Stratosphere Hotel in Las Vegas. Have you seen it? You should. It's not good. But you should. Should see it.

And then there's: Have you driven through Utah? It's astounding.

(Turner's "The Passage of St. Gothard" projected.)

Yeah, I mean, well, not like that, but, see, yeah, that's Turker, Trucker—Turner! Turner.

Did you ever do that when you were young? You'd see a painting or a large landscape or a map and you'd trace your finger along it like it was a little person? Climbing? Up and up! And then when he, you know, would fall over to his death it would scream, "Ahhhhh, ooooh my God!!! Help me!" But you try, bring him back, and— argh.

It's on my mind a lot because of the essay in—was it *New York Times? Magazine?* Or *Herper's? Harper's?* I don't remember where I read it. It's about this—oh! Yes! I do remember where I read it: I read it at the dentist office. I got a kernel stuck in my tooth, deep in the gum, the roots, and it got infected—a few weeks ago. About the sublime. There's some new exhibition, so this young, you know, cultural critic or what not, wrote a piece. Interesting stuff: all about the sublime. This philosophical, uh, historically philosophical notion. So, here: When we look at pictures like this: Caspar David Friedrich's iconic painting *Wanderer Above the Sea of Fog*, from 1818, this one. This is the image that stands out to us as ultimately sublime. Right? More so than the others of flora and fauna, as it were, because we see ourselves in this figure. Which, I guess, is a testament to the work, yes. It is not a painting, like many from this era, where the landscape simply overwhelms—no, no, no—here, we see ourselves, we are looking at ourselves looking at that which we cannot fathom. The horror, that fear, of not being able to digest it, not able to contain it with our own experiences. But what good is a painting?

The language of the sublime was planted in the landscape—

(VOICE: *Like a tree?*)

JUD (*Perturbed.*): . . . intellectually to our contemporaries this does not compute.

The landscape has been captured, not by canvas, by film. If the camera can capture the landscape, then it is dead. It has been murdered! We are no longer overwhelmed. We are no longer grazing in nature; we're just sittin' around, just sittin' around, sittin' around kinda masturbating at home.

YABBUT!

—so, so, so, what is the source of the modern sublime? We cannot address this without a posit, and that is: what began as a battle amongst the literati was ultimately won by the painter-philosopher. The aesthetic **(He keeps spitting this word, as if it were dry tobacco on his tongue.)**, the aesthetic, the aesthetic, the aesthetic of the sublime no longer has a place in our cultural lexicon: unless we want to talk about oil in the sea. Sewage in your water. Toxicity in the air. Plastic in your lungs. This is as rooted to nature as we will ever get again. That my feet are plastic, my heart is metal, and I jerk off with my left hand.

Oh, and just so you know, in the next, uh, twenty minutes, there'll be a MONSTER on this stage. But don't worry. Really. No, no, no: Jesus! That's not what I'm saying. I'm saying, don't worry, if you need me I'll be here. You can just say: JUUUUUD! That's my name. And I'll come running out and I'll say: WHAAAAT?

Except I'll try not to sound like an asshole when I do it. I'll say, quite crisply, directly, to you: Yes, what?

The sublime, the sublime, SURE, SURE, SURE, that's what we're here to talk about tonight. This is going to be more like a discussion. I'm going to say something and then you're going to say something and we're going to work through it this way. Okay. Okay. Now: let me get myself into a temper.

(SOUND: *An opera descends.***)**

I wonder. I wonder and I wonder. What if man were not the possessor of the art? Because we've got it now. We can hold the damned thing—we can hold the damned unfathomable THING in our hand, in the bathroom stall, so small, everything is diminished, so TINY. So what then? What if the sublime were the possessor of man?

I want to be the monster! I WANT TO BE THE MONSTER.

Dearest Mary Shelly, the author wrote, into INFINITY, let me be the monster, let me be the monster.

The plea went on and on this way. Let me be the monster.

The essayist, THE AUTHOR, signed his name.

PS: LET ME BE THE MONSTER!

Oh, mirror mirror on the wall. For all is just a mirror, isn't it? Give me a room with white walls, give me no paintings, when I look in the mirror, the wall, I want a clean slate, I want to stare for hours at that until my eyes are burnt clean and then only, only then give me raw meat and I'll pound it, squatting, caveman style, to oblivion.

The landscape is such a profundity, my eye is an eye, Jell-O-like, really, and I look with my Jell-O over the vast expanse of the desert, or the sea, the waterfalls, and the mountains rise, and I cannot fathom the landscape.

But, I'm bored. But, I'm bored. ButI'mBored. Buti'mbored. I'M BORED!

I can take a shot of my own backyard and it'll look better than any Degas, Ragu, Voodoo, who-do, you do. Shutup! Ba-da-bu-dup-dup daaaa! LONDON BRIDGE IS FALLING DOWN FALLING DOWN FALLING DOWN LONDON BRIDGE IS FALLING DOWN MY FAIR LADY!!!!

I know what this is.

But, I'm bored.

Duuuuuuuhhh…

But, I'm bored.

Duuuuuuuhhh…

But, I'm bored.

Duuuuuuuuhh…

This is the question. Have you met a man consumed? Have you met a consumed? I bet that man can sue. There's a boy called Sue. A man called Sue. So Sue me!

This all seems frighteningly familiar. Because this is all designed, this is a designed goddamned thing. This is not about building, but designing. Who said that? NO BODY, LEAVE IT ALONE!

THE SOUND OF A PLAY BEGINNING: DUN DUN DUN!

We must begin.

IOWA OF MY MIND

Barbara Cassidy

CHARACTER: PROFESSOR HAROLD TULINSKY, Iowa State University. forties to sixties. Convicted sex offender.

PLACE: A bare stage

CIRCUMSTANCE: Speaking to the audience.

PROFESSOR: Hello. I don't believe I have given my little personal anecdote breakfast speech, so here we go.

The most delectable breakfast I have ever had was actually in New Finland at a farmhouse I was visiting. Two exquisite poached eggs. A paper-thin sliced Canadian bacon and a home-baked thick-crusted wheat bread (warm and slathered with sweet butter). Topped off with a mimosa, how can you go wrong with that, by far the most wonderful breakfast I have ever had. Yes, of this I am certain.

This was also the day I met a certain innocent by the name of Kimberly LaCroix, a young woman-child who was serving at her mum and dad's B & B, serving this wondrous breakfast, and this was only befitting. The breakfast, the girl. I had the realization that love can come in many different ways and age did not hold any weight in the matters of the heart. It would make no sense to say I cannot fall in love with a ten-year-old when I am thirty if I then legitimately could do so in eight years when she was eighteen and I was thirty-eight. Can you see the insanity in that? Can one not see the potential in a person? Can one not see the adult in the child? I would say that possibly only an insightful person can . . . maybe that is more like it . . . A run-of-the-mill Joe could not see the beauty of the young woman in a tween . . . no . . . in any case I try to keep that experience in my mind in life as much as possible, because of the ways it affected my being. I'm probably being a tad too intimate here. Numero uno, it made me think differently about food, I daresay. Food was meant to be savored and enjoyed and good food was to be relished. Food was more than a means to nourishment and every experience with food should be made into an event. If possible. Fresh ingredients are essential. And simultaneously, I came to be able to appreciate people of all ages, especially young people. Through this young woman, I came to realize, that loving a youngster is beautiful and, indeed, quite possible and reasonable. And yes, it is with truth that I assert that this society is totally buggered, hypocritical, and without any knowledge of itself. And makes problems where they do not need to be. There are real, very real problems in the world. We could use some more thinkers and unfortunately, the middle class is the last place one looks to find thinkers. You have to look higher or lower to find the visionaries. Not as much to lose . . . not so firmly aligned with their structural positions . . . Good evening . . .

OUR LADY OF KIBEHO
Katori Hall

CHARACTER: BISHOP GAHAMANYI, town bishop, head of the Butare Diocese, Rwanda

PLACE: Father Tuyishime's office. (He is the head priest of Kibeho College, an all-girl school.) Kibeho, Rwanda, 1981–1982.

CIRCUMSTANCE: Bishop Gahamanyi reminds Father Tuyishime that he is a Tutsi, a chosen tribe; he is really seeking his support to allow an investigation from the Vatican into the alleged apparitions of the Virgin Mary in Rwanda.

BISHOP GAHAMANYI: You, Father Tuyishime, have been chosen . . . by me.

(FATHER TUYISHIME: *Am I but a figurehead?*)

BISHOP GAHAMANYI: You are truly a figure, but being a head? I'm not so sure. There is always someone above the head, above the tree, and dare I say above the sky. You must remember butter cannot fight against the sun. I understand your concern. I truly do, but if we do not allow him the space and time for an investigation we will regret it. Horribly.

(FATHER TUYISHIME: *And why is that?*)

(*Pause.*)

BISHOP GAHAMANYI: Since this all started happening there have been seven youths who claim to have visions of the Virgin Mary.

(FATHER TUYISHIME: *Seven?*)

BISHOP GAHAMANYI: Seven so-called visionaries. You remember that boy, Emmanuel, who had the sickness? Claimed that he was cured that day the sun danced? Well, now Emmanuel is saying he saw Jesus in a cornfield. Can you believe? Jesus. In a cornfield?

(FATHER TUYISHIME: *Who is to say this boy did not in fact see what he said he saw?*)

BISHOP GAHAMANYI: Jesus? In a cornfield?

(FATHER TUYISHIME: *Seems like the perfect place—*)

BISHOP GAHAMANYI: Said he had hair of knotty ropes that fell around his shoulders like a lion. And that he was a tall, wiry man wrapped in a *kitenge*. A *kitenge*? Well, Emmanuel was soon stripped naked in the streets, his clothes shredded like banana leaves before a feast. They say he has gone mad staring at the sun looking for this Jesus. He and the others are all just crazy children who have caught the religious fever, but *these* girls, these girls could make the sun shine forever on this small little village no one knows about, cares about.

(FATHER TUYISHIME: *This is a change of heart from your previous position.*)

BISHOP GAHAMANYI: Do you know how many people visited Fatima after those three little children saw the Virgin Mary?

(FATHER TUYISHIME: *No, but—*)

BISHOP GAHAMANYI: A million a year. Can you imagine a million a year descending upon Kibeho? The villagers could sell rosaries, shirts, tapes of the girls' lovely messages—

(FATHER TUYISHIME: *Our faith cannot be commodified, Bishop.*)

BISHOP GAHAMANYI: I'm not talking about commodification, I'm talking about confirmation. These girls are our only chance, and we need to help them any way we can. They are already passing the medical tests, but the liturgical ones, EN-HENH . . .

(FATHER TUYISHIME: *Alphonsine gets nervous sometimes—*)

(BISHOP GAHAMANYI *leans in. Pulls out a paper from his robe and sets it on* FATHER TUYISHIME'*s desk.*)

BISHOP GAHAMANYI: Well, sometimes even us chosen ones need some help. Make sure Alphonsine knows these answers backward and forward. She must pass the next test—

(FATHER TUYISHIME: *If she gets everything right, he will be suspicious.*)

BISHOP GAHAMANYI: Say the Virgin Mary told her the answers.

(FATHER TUYISHIME: *That would be cheating.*)

(BISHOP GAHAMANYI: *It would be studying.*)

(FATHER TUYISHIME: *So you want me to lie?*)

BISHOP GAHAMANYI: I want you to help, goddamn it! I have seen Alphonsine's grades. You would think that a Tutsi woman would have passed on better smarts to her child. You'd think she was Hutu with how stupid—

(FATHER TUYISHIME: [*Barking.*] BISHOP GAHAMANYI. [*Softening.*] *Your excellency,* [*Even softer.*] *please.*)

(*Beat.*)

BISHOP GAHAMANYI: This will be good for Kibeho. Good for the future of Rwanda.

(FATHER TUYISHIME: *The future of Rwanda?*)

BISHOP GAHAMANYI: If these girls are confirmed, and they will be confirmed, Father Tuyishime, with or without your help, they will make a name for Rwanda, a name for this village. In the future I see a shrine, taller than any tree with a steeple that scratches the belly of the clouds . . . we shall call it Our Lady of Kibeho, a church surrounded by millions, *millions* dancing with love.

AN OCTOROON

Branden Jacobs-Jenkins

CHARACTER: BJJ (as the playwright himself), a black man

PLACE: A stage

CIRCUMSTANCE: While applying whiteface at a vanity table on a folding chair.

BJJ: I believe an important part of being a good artist
is recognizing your limits.
So I can respect the pussies who pussy out of a project.
I respect it when they get their "people" to be all like,
"Well, such-and-such doesn't really get the stuff about slaves."
I'm like, "What is there not to get? It's slavery.
And I'm not even asking you to play the slaves.
You're playing the goddamn slave owner."
I mean, God forbid you ask a black guy
to play some football-playing illiterate drug addict
magical negro Iraq vet with PTSD who's
secretly on the DL with HIV but who's
also trying to get out of a generic ghetto with his
pregnant obese girlfriend who has anger-management issues
from a history of sexual abuse—
In fact, everyone's been sexually abused—
And someone's mother has a monologue
Where she's snotting out of her nose and crying everywhere

because she's been caught smoking crack
and fired from her job as a hotel maid . . .

(*Beat.*)

(I just made that up . . . Dibs.)

(*Beat.*)

God forbid any actor of color not jump at the chance
to play an offensive bag of garbage
so far from his own life
but which some idiot critic or marketing intern is going to
        describe as
a gritty, truthful portrayal of "the Black experience
in America," but the minute you ask a white guy
to play a racist whose racism isn't
"complicated" by some monologue
where he's like
"I don't mean to be racist!
It's just complicated!"
he doesn't return your phone calls?
Then my therapist was like,
"Don't you think you ought to not shit where you eat?"
and I was like,
"Well, what happens if I shit where I starve?"

**(*Playwright enters, also mostly—if not completely—naked and
standing in the back, listening.*)**

"Black playwright."
I can't even wipe my ass
without someone trying to accuse me
of deconstructing the race problem in America.

I even tried writing a play about
talking farm animals once—
just to avoid talking about people—
and this literary manager was like, "Oh my God!
You're totally deconstructing African folktales, aren't you?"
I'm like,
"No. I'm just writing about farm animals."
And she's like,
"No, no. You're totally deconstructing African folktales.
That's totally what you're doing."
And I was like, "Bitch!
I'm not fucking deconstructing
Any fucking African fucking folktales!
I'm writing a fucking play about
my issues with substance abuse
and then I am attributing the dialogue to a
fucking fox
and a fucking rabbit
to protect identities! *Fuck you!*
Give me a fucking break!"
And, by break, I mean a production.

HERMAN KLINE'S MIDLIFE CRISIS

Josh Koenigsberg

CHARACTER: HERMAN KLINE, a doctor at Mount Sinai Medical Center. Fifties, male. Often deep in thought; sick of tuning out all the loud noise around him so he can think straight.

PLACE: The rooftop of Cedars Mt. Sinai Hospital in Manhattan

CIRCUMSTANCE: Herman is accidentally locked out at the back entrance to the hospital with Ernie, a drug dealer. Herman has been carrying around a large stash of crack that he took from a dead man's rectum, which Ernie wants. He has also very recently been diagnosed with early onset Alzheimer's disease, which he just revealed to Ernie.

HERMAN: Oh, please! I cheated on my wife.

(ERNIE: *You what—?*)

HERMAN: Don't be so naïve. What, you think I was telling you about my wonderful life before?

That life is good? Well it's not, it's shit. You know what I do as soon as I wake up in the morning? I count the hours until I can go back to sleep. And so I cheated on my wife with her sister! I flew out to Boca and slept with her. And guess what? Her teeth are brown!

(ERNIE: *You're disgusting.***)**

HERMAN: You don't know the half of it! It wasn't even exciting. I sat there on the plane to Boca waiting to get laid by my wife's sister, just bored to death. Because I thought it would make me happy, give my life meaning! Well, it didn't! All it did was make me come to terms with the same truth that we all know on some level—that it's all meaningless. Everything! There's nothing out there, nothing special about us. And nothing is going to matter to me anymore soon anyway. Because I'm going to be a vegetable. So I wasn't going to do your drugs. And I wasn't going to sell them. I was going to keep them close to me and never let them go ever again. Because even when I become a vegetable, I could look at them and remember! Remember, just for a brief second who I was . . . and what it was like to be human!

NORTH TO MAINE

Brenton Lengel

CHARACTER: NICK, twenty-seven, an entrepreneur from Florida

PLACE: The Appalachian Trail, present time

CIRCUMSTANCE: Nick, a more experienced hiker, is resting with Adam, twenty-three, on the trail for the first time. He's just graduated from college.

(ADAM: *I wish I were, but I'm not that creative . . . I am a twenty-three-year-old kid trying to play "knight" in the forest. It's pathetic. I should just pack it all up and go home. Beg Steve for my job back. I need to face reality; I'm not on an adventure.*)

(*Pause.*)

NICK: Yes you are.

(ADAM *looks at him.*)

NICK: There are no wizards or orcs, but look: you are having your adventure. . . . Do you believe in God?

(ADAM: *Yeah—*)

NICK: Well, I don't, and I figure we're better off without him. It's like what Nietzsche said: in a universe without God, our lives have no inherent meaning, other than what we impose. We are the ones who make our lives great; WE take the chaos around us and mold it into something beautiful. That's what you're doing. You are on an adventure . . . that doesn't change because there are no dragons or wizards. Hell, if you ask me, you're better off without them. There's more magic in these hills, or in Picasso, or Einstein, than in all the fairies or gods ever imagined.

(ADAM: *So you're telling me I'm some sort of übermensch?*)

NICK: You're an über-nerd, but you're an über-nerd who's living life on his terms, and I think that's pretty fucking cool.

(ADAM: *Dude . . . he was cheating on her, for months. How the fuck do you do something like that? I can't even respect my own father. How can I be an adult when the very definition of it has . . .*)

NICK: That drama with your parents? It sucks and it's fucked up, but you know what? It's going to pass. That's the way life is. It's like climbing a goddamn mountain. You haul your ass up the switchbacks until your clothes are caked with salt, and your eyes are burning and blurry from the sweat, and your legs are getting ready to mutiny. You keep telling yourself that the summit is right around the next corner . . . and it's not, but you'll get there eventually. And no matter how bad it seems, and how much your muscles scream for you to stop, you can always take one more step—and when you get there, man . . . you look out over the hills and the valleys and if it's clear enough, it's like you can see forever; like you can see through time. And the future and past are stretched out before you in all directions, and you say to yourself, "I climb mountains."

THE COUNTRY HOUSE

Donald Margulies

CHARACTER: WALTER KEEGAN, sixty-six, a successful film and stage director

PLACE: Walter's country house in the Berkshires

CIRCUMSTANCE: With his brother-in-law Elliot Cooper, a failed actor and aspiring playwright.

WALTER: Grow up, Elliot. Selling out is a young person's idea. An adolescent's romantic notion that in order to be an artist you need to starve and suffer; commercial success is the devil's work. Well, I say, nuts to that.

(ELLIOT: *You were the paragon of artistic success!*)

WALTER: I was the paragon of nothing! I was a pragmatist who got sick of filling my calendar just to make enough to scrape by, and wanted to make some real money for a change!

(ELLIOT: *How does it feel knowing that you'll be best remembered for pandering to the puerile impulses of fifteen-year-old boys?*)

WALTER: It feels fine! If you think I've lost any sleep over this . . . I have nothing against fifteen-year-old boys; they're as legitimate a demographic as any. Fifteen-year-old boys have made me rich. I am indebted to them. Call it pandering if you like. I call it commerce. I provide a product to a vastly appreciative audience.

(ELLIOT: *My God. "Product." Listen to you! The old Walter would have been sick to his stomach.*)

WALTER: I *am* the old Walter. Same guy! I made this choice, long ago, no looking back, no regrets. What should I regret? The work onstage I didn't do? Not a chance. Starvation is not a virtue. I've tried it. It takes just as much energy and imagination making good, commercial entertainment than it does to make so-called art. So why not get paid for it? I discovered there will always be fifteen-year-old boys, an endless supply, *ad infinitum*, who go to the movies to watch all the cool different ways you can blow stuff up. I happen to like that too.

(ELLIOT: *But what have you contributed to the world but pollution? At least when you worked in the theater . . .*)

WALTER: Ah, the thea-tuh, the thea-tuh. If I hear one more time how I abandoned the fucking thea-tuh . . . The grandiosity of theater people! Who have convinced themselves that what they do is of a higher order than all other forms of make-believe! What an odd pursuit, when you stop to think about it: Grown people shouting in rooms missing a fourth wall?

BURNING THE OLD MAN

Kelly McAllister

CHARACTER: BOBBY, the brother who messed up

PLACE: A motel room

CIRCUMSTANCE: With his brother Marty, on a quest to spread their father's ashes over the Burning Man Festival together as he wished.

BOBBY: I had a nightmare. I woke up crying.

(MARTY: *What were you crying about?*)

BOBBY: Dad.

(MARTY: *Oh.*)

BOBBY: He was dying all over again, and I couldn't do anything to stop it. It was fucking horrible. We were all in his room; he was in bed, staring at me. I asked him what was wrong. He looked down at himself, and I saw that his crotch was soaked in blood. I was horrified—I couldn't move or speak or do anything. He kept looking at me with this sad, strange expression, like there was something I was supposed to be doing, but I couldn't figure out what it was. And then everyone in the room—all his buddies from Alaska—picked up his bed and carried him out. I tried to scream, but I couldn't make any noise. Then all his buddies came back into the room, and I knew what they were going to say, and I started crying, uncontrollably. Weird, huh?

(MARTY: *Yes.***)**

BOBBY: You remember that Figure Eight song on *School House Rock*?

(MARTY: *The ice-skating girl?***)**

BOBBY: At the end, as she circled the ice on that empty lake in the middle of nowhere, over and over, she sang, "Place it on its side, it spells infinity." That freaked me out. The first time I saw it, I asked Mom what infinity meant, and she said it was like a line in space that went on forever. No end. Just continuing on. And I was thinking just now, that if I was that line, shooting through space like a beam of light, I will never, ever, ever see Dad again. And that's fucked up.

(MARTY: *Yes, yes, it is.***)**

BOBBY: So I smoked out and now I'm a little high, and I'm trying to gather my memories, you know? Store them up for the long haul to eternity. But I'm beginning to realize that I don't remember it all. I wish I did, but I can't.

(MARTY: *Oh.***)**

BOBBY: What he was like when we were little.

(MARTY: *Who?***)**

BOBBY: Dad.

(MARTY: *Oh. He was like he was before he died, with more hair.***)**

BOBBY: I can't remember much. One time when he was shaving. I watched him put shaving cream on his face and thought it looked funny. I snuck up behind him and hit him on the ass. He got really pissed. He was shaving with that straight razor. And he yelled at me. Then he apologized and carried me around the house and told me a story. I think that's the only memory I have of Dad before he left.

LAST CALL

Kelly McAllister

CHARACTER: DAVID, thirties. Former stock broker going through an existential dilemma after 9/11

PLACE: A bar

CIRCUMSTANCE: David is explaining to his friends what happened to him and how 9/11 freaked him out.

DAVID: It was about three months after 9/11. After everyone started acting like their normal, boring, creepy selves. Especially me. Thousands of people dead. A war on terrorism that just gets curiouser and curiouser. Anthrax, some kid putting pipe bombs in mailboxes—things are totally fucked up. And here I am, buying this and selling that, closing deals like nothing ever happened. Keep going on like before. That's what everyone said to do to fight the terrorists. Keep going on like before. Even if you're an asshole, keep going on like before.

It's all so fucked and weird. You ever feel like nothing makes sense, that time and space are all warped and you're just sort of floating through it, powerless? So, one night, I go out drinking down on the Lower East Side, and I get into a fight with the bartender because he doesn't have the kind of vodka I like. I was screaming bloody murder at this guy because he didn't carry my brand. And in the middle of the argument, while I'm screaming, it hit me: I'm an asshole. And that was it, I had had enough. I walked to the nearest subway station, past beggars and drunks and dealers, past manholes puffing steam like smoke from Aladdin's lamp, down to the F train platform, and waited.

People jump all the time. I'm surprised that more people don't do it. Just to see what happens. This other guy was there. Italian suit. Cuban cigar. A little rag doll in his hands. Talking to himself, laughing, dancing around. We both hear the train coming. He looks over to me, smiles, and tosses me the doll.

I take this as a sign from God to keep on living. Then the guy jumps in front of the train.

So I got his doll, and parts of this dead guy on me. He died. I took a long, long walk. Sometime after dawn I ended up in Central Park, sitting at Bethesda Fountain, crying like a baby.

SOME UNFORTUNATE HOUR

Kelly McAllister

CHARACTER: TOM, early thirties

PLACE: A dive bar

CIRCUMSTANCE: Tom is having a really bad day. He has just signed his divorce papers, and is drinking away his sorrows in his favorite dive bar. And may be losing his mind.

TOM: It comes down to two choices, really. When you get down to it. You can either be Asshole Happy Clown, or Idiot Sad Clown.

Asshole Happy Clown is happy because he thinks people suck, that we're just a bunch of assholes. And he is constantly proved right. So he smiles, not so much because he's glad the world sucks, but because, asshole that he is, nothing makes him happier than being right. Even if it's about something terrible.

Idiot Sad Clown is the optimist of the pair. He thinks—no, believes—in the inherent goodness of people. He holds out great hope for us all. And he is continually heartbroken. People do the stupidest shit imaginable, on a constant basis—both to themselves and to each other. They lie to each other. They take advantage of each other. They don't tell you what's really going on inside, even if you ask them again and again. "What's going on?" "Nothing, everything's fine."

They leave you. With little to no explanation. They say things like, "This package was broke when you bought it," whatever the fuck that is supposed to mean. Who says shit like that? Broke when you bought it? Not only is that fucked up in its own right, it implies a belief that most of us packages aren't broken. That most of us are just fine. Which is crazy. I promise you, there are no unbroken packages. None of us are without a dent or two or twelve.

Broke when you bought it? Jesus fucking Christ! When I got married, what I had hoped for—what I prayed for, in my lapsed Irish Catholic way—the three things I was looking for in my wife were, in no particular order: faith, hope, and/or charity. What did I get? The complaint department at Sears! I got the fucking Maytag Repairman! Looking for a wife, I got some old turd telling me that he has the loneliest job on the face of the earth. Which is bullshit. The loneliest job on the face of the earth was, until this afternoon, according to a certain paper I signed down at the courthouse, held by me.

Oh my God! I'm the Maytag Repairman! I don't want to fix washing machines. I want—no, I hope—to one day be called upon to repair some lost soul. Of course, I don't know how to do that, so part of me is happy that the phone never rings down in the soul department at Sears, but still, I'd like to give it a try. Just once. And for real, not for make-up. Did you know that most of life is a game of make-up? It is. We make up these characters, these people who we'd like to be; and we spend our lives playing our ideas of ourselves. And that seems crazy to me.

Faith, hope, and charity. The three weird sisters. The three amigos. That's all.

SOME UNFORTUNATE HOUR

Kelly McAllister

CHARACTER: TOM, just divorced. Early thirties.

PLACE: A bar in Denver, Colorado

CIRCUMSTANCE: Tom has met a woman named Charity, and he is nervous.

TOM: Charity, I'm sorry. Didn't mean to freak out on you like that. I just have a lot of issues going on, and this is sort of overwhelming.

(CHARITY: *What's overwhelming?***)**

TOM: You. This. Everything. Don't tell me you don't hear the drums! The natives are restless, and we are in for some serious shit. I know I seem pretty together, but I'm not. I mean, Jesus, I saw The Elephant! So what do you expect?

(CHARITY: *The elephant?***)**

TOM: Yeah. The Elephant. (***Nature documentary music starts to play.* TOM** *narrates like a nature show host.*) Babar the Baleful. When my wife was dumping me, she told me that I needed to see the elephant. And I thought she meant The Elephant—the thing that the pioneers said they saw if they turned back home. A lot of the pioneers on their way west never made it to where they wanted to go—for lots of reasons. Tornados, rattlesnakes, birthday parties— it was a tough road, and not everybody made it. A lot of them stopped right here in Denver. They'd see the Rockies looming ahead like a huge and impenetrable fortress—like God Himself was standing before them—and He was a vengeful God. A God who saw through all their bullshit. And the Lord said, "You have failed. You lose. Turn around and walk in misery the rest of your days." And so they would—they'd just turn around and go back to where they started. Ashamed. And if their friends and family asked them in kind concerned tones what happened, all they could manage to quietly say was that they had seen The Elephant.

And so, when She Who Shall Remain Nameless said that I needed to see The Elephant, I thought that was a great analogy. We'd spent five years on a painful, hardship-filled road—and we couldn't take it. Not anymore. We weren't going to end up where we thought we were going to end up. The Lord had spoken. But He didn't say what I thought he was going to say. See, I thought my dear wife was trying to reach out to me, to help me understand what was going on. And I told her so. And she said, "No. You need to see the elephant in the room. I don't love you anymore, and I want a divorce." Good times.

SITTING DUCK SEASON

Robin Rice

CHARACTER: TUNA, thirties

PLACE: A corporate office in Manhattan

CIRCUMSTANCE: Tuna tries to get a CEO who is running from the law to face the music. He blames her for his mother's suicide. He is, in actuality, her conscience.

TUNA: Forget who I am? It's been awhile. You've made a mess, Roberta. Without me, you've run amok. Lucky for you I tracked you down.

It *is* a little much—shit on the shirt, crap on the—Did I hurt your cultivated ears? Hate to break the news, but if you don't cooperate, it's gonna get worse. I ain't leavin 'til you break. Livin' with me won't be no walk in Central Park, baby doll. No siree. I'm sure I leave the toilet seat up. Pretty certain I don't get latte or whatever the fuck at Starbucks or eat croutons or meet with hotshots in conference rooms on the 200th floor with way-down-below poor slobs like me like ants. Still—with the muck you're up to your eyeballs in . . .

I may be disgusting, but I'm your insides, baby. It's your brain that chose this nasty-ass form for me. No skin off my teeth. Never fooled myself I was pretty. I ain't a master at fooling myself like you. Better a halo that needs polishin' than no halo at all, I say.

Don't turn away. You ain't gonna rest 'til it's over. Not 'til you face what you done.

You're in a bad way. It's gotten so when you look in mirrors your eyes go blank. You switch on to automatic. D'you even remember what color your own eyes are? Not to worry. I didn't give up on you. Been biding my time in the back of your skull where you shoved me. Not dead. Oh no. Long as you breathe, I breathe. Buried under rationalizations, smothered under self-deception—but still breathing. Waiting for a chink to open. Wanting so bad to squeeze through and make you goddamn see yourself for real. See past the helmet hairdo and silk suits and eyebrows that don't move. I'm gonna make you see, baby. I'm gonna make you recognize the filth and crap I been rolling in inside you in your black soul. Before I'm through you're gonna shake hands with yourself. Today is Happy Face-the-Music Day. Listen up.

HOUSE OF TRASH

Trav S.D.

CHARACTER: BOB—a middle-age preacher

PLACE: Outside a run-down rural house

CIRCUMSTANCE: Speaking to his son upon discovering his nephew is in the barn with a young woman.

BOB: Well, you told me now. That's the important thing. Well, he's got the gall bringing that woman over here, that's all I can say. His twenty-five-year-old concubine, so they can have their roll in the hay over to Grandpa's place. Hey? Like this is the "Sex Motel," House of a preacher? They're out there fornicating like a couple of half-baked jackrabbits. Say! What'd you let 'em do a thing like that for, anyhow? Lettin' the two of them fornicate out there like a couple of half-baked jackrabbits?

(TOBY *opens his mouth to talk—*)

Strong arm ya, did they? Knowin' Pubert, he probably pulled a knife on ya. Sure. Big knife. Six-inch bowie knife. He got a knife like that. I give it to him for Christmas. He do that to ya?

(TOBY *opens his mouth to talk—*)

Lord forgive that boy. Lord forgive that monstrous, wild boy. Imagine a thing like that. Usin' a knife like that on his own uncle. A six-inch bowie knife that's for huntin' and fishin' and a-scrapin' rust off the tractor to commit violence against his own kin. He'll answer for that, I can tell ya. He was drinkin', I suppose.

(TOBY *opens his mouth to talk—*)

Oh, I can see the whole thing, in living color. Drunk on Wild Turkey. So blind drunk he can hardly stand. High on that coke too. The two of them. Out of their minds, insensible—reckless. So much so that they stop off at Grandpa's, one door over from Hayseed's farm so they can go for a roll in the hay, so doped up they can't hardly stand. That hayloft air—I know it. It's like another drug itself. Thick, sweet, hot, moist. Goes right to the head. Sure, I remember. Your eyes get watery and irritated up there. Your nostrils get greedy for it, open right up wide. Skin gets all flush, excited. And it's hot up there in that hayloft! Hundred and five degrees. You work up a sweat not doin' nothin'. Just standin' there. Just standin' there not doin' nothin'. Just talkin. Talkin' about nothing'. So you're not doin' nothing, just standin' there not doin' nothin' and ya ain't talkin' about nothing. Just nothin'. That's all yer talkin' about. Nothin'! It's a game you play, the two of ya. Neither one's thinkin' about the words. Just waitin' to see how it'll happen. Who'll hop on who. Heart's just thumpin', man. Like there's a little guy bangin' on the inside of your chest, yellin', "Let me out!" And the two of you, you're drunk on Wild Turkey, so you just gotta kinda stumble into her, and the two of you, you just go, tumblin' gentle into the hay, laughing and kissin' them whiskey-flavored kisses. That's how it happens. Bury your face in her sweaty neck there, and just kinda sloppily slidin' your mouth up and down from her ear to her shoulder. Just like eatin' watermelon. Once you get down on that shoulder, boy, why, it's only a matter of time afore she unbuttons her damn shirt herself. You don't have to do a thing, don't have to think about a thing. Your body does the whole trick itself. Your mind don't have to move a muscle. Soon her jeans are slidin' down them sweaty slim legs, boy. By God, she's a woman, boy! WHHOOOOEEEE! YEAH! Lookee that! Hell! She don't have to tell you twice. When you're eighteen, there ain't no amount of whiskey gonna make Johnny fall down. So you git on in there and ya, ya DO YOUR BIDNESS! YES, SIR!!!

*(In his excitement, **BOB** fires the shotgun off in the air. There is a startled pause as the report from the rifle fades to silence.)*

BOB: *(A little embarrassed.)* I'd better get out there and put a stop to this thing before them two kids give me a heart attack! Here, hold this.

*(**BOB** gives the gun to **TOBY** and heads offstage.)*

NOT TO BE NEGATIVE BUT . . .

Jack Sundmacher

CHARACTER: JACK, thirties–forties

PLACE: A stage

CIRCUMSTANCE: Speaking alternately to his sperm in a glass jar and to the audience.

JACK: It was May 23rd, 2005, I came home one day from passing out movie passes, I turned on the TV and walked into the kitchen to make some Cheerios, all of a sudden I heard Oprah say, "He's in the building!" The women were going crazy. I sat on my couch with my Cheerios and for the next hour I was transported back to my childhood. I started remembering how happy I was as a kid. Every Saturday morning I woke up so excited, I couldn't wait to watch *Super Friends*. It's a bird, it's a plane, it's Tom Cruise. And he came out wearing all black. Oprah thanked him for coming to her ball. I thought to myself, what's a ball? And she said, "Wasn't that great?"

And Tom said, "It was more than great, it was more than fun, it was historic."

(JACK *talks to audience*.)

I've had fun nights, I've even had a couple great nights, but I've never had a historic night.

And Oprah said, "What has happened to you?"

(JACK *imitates Tom Cruise. He raises both hands in the air, then one hand in the air.*)

And then Tom said, "That's how I feel about it."

(JACK *goes down on one knee.*)

Oprah said, "Something has happened to you?"

Tom said, "I'm in love."

Oprah said, "We've never seen you like this before?"

(JACK *jumps on a couch.*)

Oprah said, "You're gone, the boy is gone."

I thought to myself, no, Oprah, he's not gone, you're gone. He's expressing himself. He's in love. Tom's not human, Oprah. He doesn't express love like humans do. You can't hold him to the same standards. Don't you understand, Oprah, he's not one of us. He's better. He's free. When Tom jumped, he jumped for all of us. He's not afraid of being judged, he does what he wants. Great white sharks don't ask for permission to jump. They jump and all the other fish get out of the way. Guppies don't jump. They're scared they'll be eaten alive.

Oprah said, "You've never had this type of feeling."

Tom said, "I'm not going to pretend."

He wasn't telling Oprah that, he was telling me that. He's been with me my whole life. And now he was on *Oprah* talking to me, telling me to stop pretending your life is fine, stop pretending you like passing out movie passes, stop pretending you don't want to be me.

(*Fantasy music.*)

I started imagining a day in the life of Tom Cruise. He wakes up, brushes his big shark teeth, runs around his private track, pumps iron, pops some vitamins, takes a shower, has sex with whoever is next to him, reads a chapter of *Dianetics*, gives his team their assignments for the day, calls Oprah to say hi, flies his plane around town, lands on top of the Four Seasons hotel, meets Spielberg for lunch, gives him a massage, gets back on his plane, lands at the Tom Cruise airport, located in his backyard, brushes his big shark teeth, rides his motorcycle to Malibu to the soundtrack of *Top Gun*. Asks whoever is next to him to come with him to Mexico for breakfast. On the way back to Los Angeles, gives CPR to a kid who was hit by a car. Reads another chapter of *Dianetics*. Brushes his big shark teeth. Calls Spielberg to say good night.

You guessed it. Scientology, here I come. Before I knew it, I was walking up the bridge. The bridge is a chart that outlines a series of steps one must take in sequence to reach the highest levels of awareness.

(*Sound cue:* Close Encounters of the Third Kind *theme song.*)

I drove to a place called the Celebrity Center. Even the name sounds fantastic. I get to hang out with celebrities. Hey, Travolta, get over here. Hey, Kirstie Alley, what's up, girl? Are you still doing that sitcom? You're so brilliant. Speaking of brilliant, Giovanni Ribisi, what's up, my man? Juliette Lewis, how are you? You guys want to play Twister or something? We're having a game night soon. You should all come. If you see Tom, tell him I'm looking for him. Alright, you guys.

NOT TO BE NEGATIVE BUT . . .

Jack Sundmacher

CHARACTER: JACK, thirties–forties

PLACE: A stage

CIRCUMSTANCE: Speaking to his sperm that he calls Hope, that he keeps in a glass jar.

(JACK's *wife calls*.)

JACK: That's my wife. We're going to the fertility clinic. I have to go. If you make it out of there I will be your father. That's one of the crappy things about life, you can't choose your parents. You'll think I'm the best dad in the world for a long time until your mother makes you see a therapist and then you'll realize I wasn't so great. The therapist will tell you all the mistakes I made and how I wasn't loved like I should be and that's why I can't love you the way you should be and all that will be true. I will be paying for this therapist to make you hate me. And you'll hate me. That's good. You'll be feeling. It doesn't matter what the feeling is, just feel, that's all. All feelings are good. No feelings are bad. Don't worry if you hate me. You'll love me later when I tell you I have cancer. And you'll try to raise money for radiation treatments. Don't do it. Keep your money because I won't have any to give you when I die because I gave it all to the therapist.

One more thing, here are my words of wisdom. Take it or leave it. A lot of my life has been trying to figure out life. It can't be figured out. I've used confusion as a way of staying safe. It's not confusion, it's fear. Fear is really smart, smarter than me. It's kicked my ass my whole life. But I didn't even know I was fighting it. It disguises itself as different things, confusion, boredom, hunger, masturbation. It's all fear. You're either staring at fear, eating fear, or fear is coming out of your penis. Don't think. Fear wants you to think. Fear will make you negative as well. I wasn't born negative. The older you get the closer you get to death and that's scary. I don't like being scared. If I got present with the fact that I'm dying, I would hug everyone all the time and tell everyone how much I love them.

Even the most mundane things would be great. An elevator ride with three other people and all three people know they're going to die. We would hug each other and try to make each other laugh. The fourteen seconds it takes to get from the lobby to the sixth floor would be amazing.

I'm sorry, I can't be positive for very long, my back starts to hurt. If we lived in a world where people hugged each other in an elevator I would be dead by the time it reached the sixth floor. Suicide. I don't know how I would kill myself but I would figure it out. The image of a stranger in an elevator telling me I'm wonderful makes me want to die. That's hell. So I guess heaven is the way it is now. Awkward silence, no eye contact, and hoping the elevator doesn't get stuck.

What I'm trying to tell you is life is about how you see things. What if life was an elevator ride? You start out at the bottom and it's up to you what kind of person you want to be while you go up. Do you want to be closed off and negative or open and positive? It's up to you. I prefer being closed off and negative but if you want to put yourself out there and create new experiences, take risks, love openly, no matter the consequences, I can't stop you. I don't recommend it but it's your life. I'll love you no matter what.

Right now it's the bottom of the ninth inning, Hope. Full count, bases loaded, and you're up. What's the worst thing you can do? It's not striking out. That's half correct. It's only bad if you strike out looking. If you see an egg, don't watch it. Take a swing. What's the worst thing that could happen? You don't become a human being. You're not missing much. It's a lot of crap you have to deal with to have maybe ten wonderful moments, and even those moments are not really wonderful. They're only wonderful later when we remember them or tell them to a friend who we want to make feel bad. When people tell you they're having so many wonderful moments, they are lying, they're not. They've just rewritten the moment to be wonderful because the older you get the more you look back, and the more you look back the more you want to see wonderful moments even though they never happened. I'll never tell you you're special, or unique, or lucky, you're not. You're a human being, you're no better or worse. You're just like everybody else trying to make sense of this terrible script that you have been forced to play a role in.

Not to be negative but. . . . even though I believe in what I just said, I still have hope that tomorrow will be better. Even though it probably won't.

PRETTY THEFT
Adam Szymkowicz

CHARACTER: BOBBY, early twenties

PLACE: The group home where Bobby's girlfriend, Allegra, works as an aide

CIRCUMSTANCE: Unbeknownst to Allegra, Bobby has just kissed Allegra's friend Suzy. Bobby will be going away to college in September.

BOBBY (*To* ALLEGRA.): Listen, we gotta talk.

(ALLEGRA: *Thank God. I need someone to talk to.*)

(BOBBY: *Not in front of the retard.*)

(ALLEGRA: *He's not . . . Joe, will you go find Melody, please.*)

(JOE *gets up and exits.*)

BOBBY: It's just . . .

(ALLEGRA: *The funeral's tomorrow.*)

BOBBY: We'll be going to different schools.

(ALLEGRA: *What?*)

BOBBY: I don't know. Maybe it's not such a good idea.

(ALLEGRA: *What's not a good idea?***)**

BOBBY: Us staying together.

(ALLEGRA: *You just thought of this?***)**

BOBBY: Yeah.

(ALLEGRA: *Today?***)**

BOBBY: You always want me to tell you how I feel. These are my feelings. Don't you want to hear about them?

(ALLEGRA: *Your feelings?***)**

BOBBY: Yeah.

(ALLEGRA: *What feelings?***)**

BOBBY: Well, you know. I been thinking.

(ALLEGRA: *You don't love me. I'm no good.***)**

BOBBY: No, it's just . . .

(ALLEGRA: *You don't want me.***)**

(BOBBY: *No, it's not that.***)**

BOBBY: It's just . . . We're young. I want to fuck other girls. I want to be free to do that at school. There's lots of different kinds of girls out there and most of them I've never even kissed. I'm sorry. Now you're mad at me.

(ALLEGRA: *What are you talking about?***)**

BOBBY: You know, girls with longer legs, or bigger breasts. Blondes, brunettes, redheads, like girls who play field hockey. Um, girls who wear those shirts that show their stomachs, uh . . . girls—

(ALLEGRA: *So we're taking a break?*)

(BOBBY: *Yeah, you can call it that if you want.*)

BOBBY: I just really need to experience lots of stuff, you know, like other girls. Hopefully lots of other girls. You know, while I'm still attractive.

(ALLEGRA: *Wow.*)

BOBBY: Yeah.

PRETTY THEFT

Adam Szymkowicz

CHARACTER: JOE, twenties–thirties. Joe is "slow" and lives in a group home.

PLACE: In a spotlight onstage

CIRCUMSTANCE: Joe speaks to the audience. He is in a straightjacket after kissing an eighteen-year-old staff aide, Allegra.

JOE: Some people get locked up and some people never do. If you try to kiss the staff they will lock you up. It is illegal. Many men in suits never go to jail. That's because that's because that's because they aren't me. They aren't broken. They walk on the surface of the water while everyone else is stuck in traffic or your car breaks down. Their cars never break down. They are super untouchable. They get married, they have wives and children because they are men that are not born broken. They are the people who are up on the big screen. They are on the TV, on the radio, in the newspaper because they are the chosen, the good, the other people. They can kiss whoever they want or kill even. Even kill. Because they are uncatchable or they are forgivable or they are perfect. They have people lying to help them. Their mothers loved them and told them so. Their mothers helped them up the stairs. Their mothers had a lot of money and a lot of good things in their bodies that they passed on while they lived in their good homes. They were beautiful and rich and were friends with all the people you are supposed to be friends with. Like doctors who can lie for you. Like doctors who can fix you. Except they don't need fixing. Not the super untouchable. They have legs like razors and eyes that magnetize. They are pretty. They are everything. Like Allegra. I wonder if Allegra is super untouchable. . . .

RARE BIRDS

Adam Szymkowicz

CHARACTER: EVAN WILLS. Sixteen, small for his age, eccentric.

PLACE: Evan's bedroom in his suburban house outside Hartford, CT

CIRCUMSTANCE: Evan is alone in his bedroom trying to take a video of himself to send to a girl he likes. Evan has never even kissed a girl.

(*EVAN sits in front of his computer. He is trying to tape a video for* JENNY. *We see the video he's making in real time project behind him.*)

EVAN: Hi, Jenny. Here's a video just for you. A sexy video. I'm . . . not wearing any underwear. No.

(*He stops taping. Starts over.*) Hi Jenny. (*Blows her a kiss.*) No.

(*Stops tape, starts over.*) Let's do this. Hi, Jenny. (*He takes off his shirt.*) There. That's better. Nobody gets to see me like this except in the gym locker room. No.

(*Stops tape. Takes off the rest of his clothes. Starts over. The video just shows him from the waist up.*) If I'm going to do this, I'm going to do this. This is me. All of me. I'm not holding anything back, Jenny. I will show you my soul. Because I feel like you have shown me yours and it's beautiful. You know, I like birds because they float above us without effort. You're like that too, Jenny. I wrote you this poem. Okay, yeah. I'm just going to read it.

(***Reads from paper.***)

Jenny Monroe
when you move
all the world stops
to watch you sail past
a vision in a tank top and jeans
and where you stop
everyone fumbles with their hands
and their hearts and nervous systems go into shock
and when your eyes fall on us lucky few
we feel the blessing of your gaze
but it's like we're standing in front of the whole school
and everyone is waiting for us to fall over
You make me fall over
Twenty times a day
I love you
Jenny.

RARE BIRDS

Adam Szymkowicz

CHARACTER: EVAN WILLS. Sixteen, small for his age, eccentric.

PLACE: Evan's bedroom in his suburban house outside Hartford, CT

CIRCUMSTANCE: Evan has been bullied at school after a video to a girl went viral. He is now alone in his bedroom with a handgun.

(EVAN *gets to a bad place in his head. He goes to his laptop, films himself. He is projected much larger on the back wall, like before.***)**

EVAN: Okay. So I guess this is it. I always thought—well, that doesn't matter. I always thought somehow someday I would figure out what I'm good for. But . . . now . . . it's clear I'm not good for anything.

I guess I should say don't blame yourself. This isn't your fault. No, fuck it. If you feel a little bit sorry for me at all, it is your fault. It's everyone's fault. It's my father's fault. Mom, this is your fault. Everyone at school, all the students, all the teachers, the principal, this is all your fault. I want the guilt to eat you up. I want you to wonder what you should have done for the rest of your life.

(Pause.)

What am I talking about? No one will miss me. No one will care. No one will feel bad. You will all be happier.

I could never fit in. I'm too weird. And that's not going to change. I can't not be who I am. I wouldn't know how.

So, I guess I'll never get to kiss a girl. I will never see a red-crowned crane in the wild. But what's the point of that anyway? It's just a fucking bird, right? No one cares about fucking birds.

I'm sorry for being in your lives, for wasting your time.

Okay. This is it. Goodbye. In my next life, I would like to be a bird. If requests are allowed. So long.

(**EVAN** *raises the gun to his head. Another beat.*)

WHEN JANUARY FEELS LIKE SUMMER

Cori Thomas

CHARACTER: DEVAUN, twenty, typical urban guy. Has a big heart.

PLACE: Devaun's house

CIRCUMSTANCE: Devaun is making signs to warn about a sexual predator in his neighborhood, helped by his friend Jeron.

DEVAUN: I'm gon' be rich and important like Derek Jeter or someone like that one day. Then I'm gon' be with my homeys, yeh yeh, me and they be chillin' in my crib on my skin couch and leopard rug. Music be playin' for the mood. You like to say I'm slow, Jeron. I ain't slow. I'm thoughtful on the question and the plan.

(JERON: *You see all these signs you got me fixin'?* [*Finishing touches.*] *This is a day's work you got me doing. You owe me.*)

(DEVAUN: *OVERTIME! Snap!*)

(*They laugh and slap five, etc.***)**

(JERON: *You better pay up, sucka.*)

DEVAUN: This is good what we doin', right, Jeron?

(JERON: *What do you mean?*)

DEVAUN: I mean how we warnin' people and shit. I want to . . . I want to . . . do something, you know, like them posters of Malcolm and Martin or Superman?

(JERON: *What?*)

DEVAUN: And I wanna teach people wrong from right or somethin' like that. But not like in church, 'cause that shit is borin' and it last too long, and the singin' is wack. But I do like it when Reverend Buford start to clear his throat three or four times in a row, like this. (*Shows him.*) And start walkin' back and forth, and speakin' forcible, and his shoulders start goin' up and down like this. (*Shows him.*) And he start swingin' one hand with his knees bended. "Yes ah," and the people in the church look like they froze up listenin'. Yeh see, that's what I like to see. How they can listen to that one man and he short and light skinned and plain till he open up his mouth and start speaking forcible. Then it's like he a new man. Like he grew or somethin'. I study that shit, 'cause I like the idea. But it don't have to be in no church. It could be anywhere. I could just say somethin' in a corner in the street, and people will stop to listen and wave they hands 'cause in that moment it will be like they feelin' the spirit of the lord or the mighty. If I can figure out how you could get people to sit on a wood bench till they ass burn listening to me. That's when I know I will become a dude with wimmins lining up and down the block waitin' for me. I will walk down the street, and birds will stop flyin' and hang in the sky and look down at me like this. (*Shows him.*) Cats, dogs, raccoon, and wimmins and everyone. Just lookin'. At me. Like this. (*Shows him.*) Like, this thing we doin' to protect the people from Lorrance is helpful and important. It's a good thing, Jeron, I can feel it. Can't you?

(JERON: *Yeh, we doin' it for the people's safety and good.*)

DEVAUN: I just want to help the world. I'm looking for the beginning moment to show people the real meaning inside of me so they can say "Whaaat?" I just want to do something for everyone to know that when we walk down the street and sidewalk, we not invisible.

WHEN JANUARY FEELS LIKE SUMMER

Cori Thomas

CHARACTER: JOE, thirties–fifties. He is a garbage man.

PLACE: A hospital room

CIRCUMSTANCE: Joe has come to keep Nirmala company as she visits her husband, who is on life support. He is attracted to her, and wasn't aware that she was married. Nirmala is facing the decision if and when to "pull the plug" and end life support.

JOE: I've been thinking about how things end up in the garbage, 'cause there's a chain of events that has to take place. First, you gotta determine if it's broken or outlived its usefulness. Then it's got to be sorted and put in the right bag. After you've done that, people like me come and pick it up. Once we've done the house to house and the truck is filled—and it can hold the ten, twenty thousand pounds or so, you and your partner picked up. And it's a dangerous job. People don't always think about wrapping things right. If you don't wear your gloves, if you don't look at what you about to pick up before you actually do, even if you do, you can get hurt. Cut by rusted metal, burned by all kinds of putrefying substances. But I'm not just talking about garbage you find in the street 'cause it was thrown out. Janice, my ex, for instance . . . we had ourselves some nice times, seemed to want the same things . . .

But seem like I had just barely got my tuxedo off and climbed into the bed to warm it up for my new wife. I had just finished exhaling a breath of relief because now I was a man with a job what's got benefits and a pension, and stability; a breath carrying with it the fact I was now looking forward to a future with my wife I could see myself enjoying . . . babies and children and a house and . . . a life. A real life . . . I should have known that something was broke that no account of trying was going to fix. I could have saved myself a lot of time . . . years full of trouble. I could have stopped holding on to my dreams so tight they had to be pried from my hands still trying and trying to hold on to them . . . Every time she came out after staying too long in the bathroom. I should have known because she always seemed nervous and couldn't settle down, and started going out and staying late . . . and . . . in and out of rehab and finally she run off and took all the savings. The minute I realized she was using that powder, I should have known that she was garbage and just accepted it. That experience made me feel that maybe because of my job, there's something in me that's gonna attract garbage, even though it's the opposite of what I want, because I want jewels, I want gold and treasure, but seem like I'm scared to try again to look for it. I'm just scared now. But when I see you tending to the store, I want to pick you up . . . and handle you carefully because you're so beautiful. You're like a flower, you're like that gold earring I saw shining on the sidewalk last Thursday. Shining in the dirt, and I couldn't help but reach down and pick it up to see if it was real. I didn't know you were married. But I do know that I want . . . I want to be here for you.

WHEN JANUARY FEELS LIKE SUMMER

Cori Thomas

CHARACTER: JERON, nineteen, typical urban kid

PLACE: His friend Devaun's house, another typical urban kid

CIRCUMSTANCE: Devaun has told Jeron a girl was interested in him, and advised him to call her. Jeron did, without much success. Devaun has just asked him how the call went.

JERON: No, I dial. She answer. I say "Hi, is this Larissa Shang?" And that's another thing, that name you gave me is wrong. Larissa Shang don't sound like Lucy Ming, Devaun. The woman's name is Lucy. So the shit was confusing right there at the jump point.

(DEVAUN: *It sound confusing the way she say it to me.*)

JERON: She say, "Who?" I tell her I got the number from you. She say "yeh?" I say "yeh." She say, "My name is Lucy." I say, "Oh." I want to punch you in your mouth right then. But then, she ask me how it feel to be on TV? So, I say "it's cool. I'm kinda like a celebrity. Do you want to git wit me?" And then I hear some quiet silence so that I can hear her breathe over the phone. But I remember how you said to keep talkin' and to put your interests up front and shit, so I ax her again forcefully if she want to git wit me. She silent. I don't know if maybe she don't speak English good or she slow, but then she say, "what do you mean?" So I say, "what do you mean, what do I mean?" She say, "What. Do. You. Mean?" In a real nasty tone. So I say, "I mean git wit me. To git. Wit. Me. Git it? You know about that, right? 'Cause if your moms and pops ain't git together, you and all human beings might not be born." So I repeat it one more time, I say, "Do. You. Want. To. Git. Wit. Me?" That's when Lucy Ming scream "I'MA SEND SOMEONE TO FUCK YOU UP!" in my ear so loud it vibrate like a bell was ringing inside my head. But then, she hang the muthafuckin' phone up on me. And when I call back, she hang up soon as I said "Hello." And this right here is exactly why I don't like to do this shit. Wimmin is stupid. Some of 'em git pregnant and you gotta spend alla your lil money on Pampers. Then some of 'em want for you to pay for them to do they nails every week. Why I want to spend my money on they nails? For what? I got more important things in the world to think about. I don't need to be talkin' on no phone to no stupid-ass punk-ass Lucy Ming. That's on you, telling me some lie on her. That girl ain't interested in me. And you made me call her like a damn stupid-ass fool. I oughta whup you, Devaun. I oughta whup your fuckin' ass.

(DEVAUN: *First of all, if you use rubbers, they won't git pregnant. Jameeraquoin tell me his girlfriend git pregnant and he was using the rubbers faithfully, so he belee she might have cut some lil holes in it first, because otherwise that shit is not humanly possible. Secondly—)*

JERON: My pops warned me to stay away from wimmin, 'cause they will tie you to the wall and suck your last drop of blood if you let 'em and you won't even know it's happenin' till it's too late and you're dried up like a branch from an old tree. Then he said to me, "You need to make sure you stay rooted in the ground, boy. Keep your leaves green. Let the sun and the rain reach your roots so you can grow tall and strong." He told me that shit expressively and looked straight into my eyes while he said it and it was the last thing he said to me . . .

THE AS IF BODY LOOP

Ken Weitzman

CHARACTER: MARTIN, mid-thirties to mid-forties

PLACE: A diner

CIRCUMSTANCE: Martin's wife was killed in the World Trade Towers on 9/11. Now, about a year after, he's reporting to Aaron (posing as a kind of therapist) what happened on the first job interview he's had since the event.

MARTIN: I knocked everything off the guy's desk. Stormed out of his office.

But you're right. I did well before that.

That stupid flag thing of yours. It worked. I was tempted. I was. They gave me the same stupid questions, the "are you sure you're sufficiently recovered to handle full-time employment?" I was pissed off, but that yellow flag. I thought about you saying "Illegal use of the tongue." So damn stupid it made me smile.

Yeah. Right up until the guy started in about my arrest.

What, they didn't tell you I was a violent criminal?

Don't worry, I wasn't convicted. I don't have a record. The thing was settled out of court. So I can truthfully answer no to the "were you ever convicted of a crime" thing. But this guy, he pressed the issue, asked me if I was ever arrested. Said, in the interest of the company it was fair to ask. Fair. That word coming from his smug mouth, it—did something to me. "Wanna hear about it?" I asked him. "It won't take long." I don't know, maybe I wanted to hit that sled, knock his question back into . . .

There I am, I say. I try to make the story dramatic for him. Give him his money's worth. *There I am*, in the supermarket. Gristedes. Doing some shopping before school. My wife was at work already. Windows on the World. She's a pastry chef. Gets there at 5 a.m. to start baking. Anyway, I'm in the frozen food aisle, running late, it's five to 9, my first class is 9:30, when Annie calls. This I find annoying because I know she's calling to check on me. She doesn't trust me to do the shopping. Even though she gives me a very explicit list. According to her, I still always miss something crucial or buy the wrong brand of something. So, because I'm annoyed and because I'm running late, I decide to . . . screen her call. I know this will irritate her and that particular morning it gave me a feeling of vindictive satisfaction.

(*Beat.*)

She didn't . . . she didn't leave a voicemail. When she called.

(*Small beat.*)

Now our friendly interviewer, he's a little uncomfortable, so I skip ahead, and spare him some of the more grisly details of the days immediately following.

So I tell him that after some time I found myself alone in my apartment, our apartment, one day, staring into an empty refrigerator. And, I don't know, maybe the thought of ordering Chinese on Christmas Day was too depressing, but I decided I would go shopping. A sign of health, a grief counselor might say. A sign of health. So like the dependent child I was when it came to food, I brought Annie's list with me. The last note she wrote me. Our final correspondence. Romantic, yes?

Organic sour cream, organic heavy whipping cream, organic peaches, organic frozen cherries, frozen waffles. "Which brings us to the climax of this particular story." *Frozen waffles*. I like them. I know, frozen waffles are an odd item to be on a pastry chef's grocery list. But I like them. The really nasty Eggo kind especially. Made Annie crazy to see me eat them for breakfast. But she put them on the list. For me. And so I kept eating them, every morning, even when I was sick of them. Because seeing her exasperated was so damn charming, and because I loved the fact that, despite that, she put it on the list every time.

But now, there I am at the market, in the frozen food section, and there are no Eggo waffles in sight. They were out of them. And, well, that was unacceptable to me. Because Annie put it on the list. And that list had come to be very important to me.

So I ask an employee to look in the back to see if any have come in that haven't made it to the shelf. But they don't want to do that. Restocking doesn't happen for another hour and a half. UNAC-CEPTABLE! I say in a voice that was a bit too loud. Perhaps a bit too belligerent. So the employee gets the manager, who apparently, at the Gristedes School of Management, did not major in customer relations. Because instead of just telling his employee to go back and get me a box of Eggo frozen waffles, recommends another brand instead. And then in a sudden burst of jocular inspiration he advises me to "leggo those Eggos."

I was unable to provide the manager with the response I believe he was looking for. Unless "if you don't go back there and get me a box of Eggos I'm going to tear out your trachea" was in fact the desired response. But judging by the fact that he called over his security guard and several other employees for backup . . .

Anyway, long story made shorter, some mostly minor injuries occurred when I tried to storm the supply room.

CREDITS AND PERMISSIONS

Communications Group. Used by permission of Derek Zasky, William Morris Endeavor Entertainment, 1325 Avenue of the Americas, New York, NY, 10019.

OFEM by Anne Hamilton. Copyright © 2016. Inquiries concerning rights should be addressed to hamiltonlit@gmail.com.

(O)n the 5:31 by Mando Alvarado. Copyright © 2010 by Mando Alvarado. Inquiries concerning rights should be addressed to ICM Partners at aorton@icmpartners.com.

Our Lady of Kibeho by Katori Hall. Copyright © 2014 by Katori Hall. From *The Best Plays of 2014*. Inquiries concerning rights should be addressed to www.katorihall.com.

Out of Focus by Geralyn Cassidy. Copyright © 2015 by Geralyn Cassidy. Inquiries concerning rights should be addressed to geralyncassidy@gmail.com or www.geralyncassidy.com.

Pretty Theft by Adam Szymkowicz. Copyright © 2009 by Adam Szymkowicz. CAUTION: Professionals and amateurs are hereby warned that *Pretty Theft* being fully protected under the copyright laws of the United States of America, the British Commonwealth countries, including Canada, and the other countries of the Copyright Union, is subject to royalty. All rights, including professional, amateur, motion picture, recitation, public reading, radio, television and cable broadcasting, and the rights of translation into foreign languages are strictly reserved. Any inquiry regarding the availability of performance rights, or the purchase of individual copies of the authorized acting edition, must be directed to Samuel French Inc., 235 Park Avenue South, 5th Floor New York, NY 10003, with other locations in Hollywood and London.

Queen for a Day by Robin Rice. Copyright © 1993, 1994 by Robin Rice. Inquiries concerning rights should be addressed to RobinRiceNYC@gmail.com or www.robinriceplaywright.com.

Rare Birds by Adam Szymkowicz. Copyright © 2017 by Adam Szymkowicz. Inquiries concerning rights should be addressed to Seth Glewen at sglewen@gershny.com.

Monologue and Scene Books

Best Contemporary Monologues for Kids Ages 7-15
edited by Lawrence Harbison
9781495011771 ....$16.99

Best Contemporary Monologues for Men 18-35
edited by Lawrence Harbison
9781480369610 ....$16.99

Best Contemporary Monologues for Women 18-35
edited by Lawrence Harbison
9781480369627 ....$16.99

Best Monologues from The Best American Short Plays, Volume Three
edited by William W. Demastes
9781480397408 ....$19.99

Best Monologues from The Best American Short Plays, Volume Two
edited by William W. Demastes
9781480385481 ....$19.99

Best Monologues from The Best American Short Plays, Volume One
edited by William W. Demastes
9781480331556 ....$19.99

Prices, contents, and availability subject to change without notice.

The Best Scenes for Kids Ages 7-15
edited by Lawrence Harbison
9781495011795 ....$16.99

Break the Rules and Get the Part
Thirty Monologues for Women
by Lira Kellerman
9781495075414..........................$12.99

Childsplay
A Collection of Scenes and Monologues for Children
edited by Kerry Muir
9780879101886 ....$16.99

Contemporary Monologues for Twentysomethings
edited by Jessica Bashline
9781495064852..........................$16.99

Contemporary Scenes for Twentysomethings
edited by Jessica Bashline
9781495065446..........................$16.99

Duo!: The Best Scenes for Mature Actors
edited by Stephen Fife
9781480360204 ....$19.99

Duo!: The Best Scenes for Two for the 21st Century
edited by Joyce E. Henry, Rebecca Dunn Jaroff, and Bob Shuman
9781557837028 ....$19.99

Duo!: Best Scenes for the 90's
edited by John Horvath, Lavonne Mueller, and Jack Temchin
9781557830302 ....$18.99

In Performance: Contemporary Monologues for Teens
by JV Mercanti
9781480396616 ....$16.99

In Performance: Contemporary Monologues for Men and Women Late Teens to Twenties
by JV Mercanti
9781480331570 ....$18.99

In Performance: Contemporary Monologues for Men and Women Late Twenties to Thirties
by JV Mercanti
9781480367470 ....$16.99

In Performance: Contemporary Monologues for Men and Women Late Thirties to Forties
by JV Mercanti
9781480396623..........................$16.99

Kids' Comedic Monologues That Are Actually Funny
by Alisha Gaddis
9781495011764............................$14.99

LGBTQ Comedic Monologues That Are Actually Funny
by Alisha Gaddis
9781495025150............................$14.99

Later Chapters
The Best Monologues and Scenes for Actors Over Fifty
edited by Diana Amsterdam
9781495072475............................$16.99

Men's Comedic Monologues That Are Actually Funny
edited by Alisha Gaddis
9781480396814 ....$14.99

One on One: The Best Men's Monologues for the 21st Century
edited by Joyce E. Henry, Rebecca Dunn Jaroff, and Bob Shuman
9781557837011 ....$18.99

Nothing Untoward
Stories from "The Pumpkin Pie Show"
by Clay McLeod Chapman
9781495061042............................$19.99

One on One: The Best Women's Monologues for the 21st Century
edited by Joyce E. Henry, Rebecca Dunn Jaroff, and Bob Shuman
9781557837004 ....$18.99

One on One: The Best Men's Monologues for the Nineties
edited by Jack Temchin
9781557831514 ....$12.95

One on One: The Best Women's Monologues for the Nineties
edited by Jack Temchin
9781557831521 ....$11.95

One on One: Playing with a Purpose
Monologues for Kids Ages 7-15
edited by Stephen Fife and Bob Shuman with contributing editors Eloise Rollins-Fife and Marit Shuman
9/81557838414 ....$16.99

One on One: The Best Monologues for Mature Actors
edited by Stephen Fife
9781480360198 ....$19.99

Scenes and Monologues of Spiritual Experience from the Best Contemporary Plays
edited by Roger Ellis
9781480331563 ....$19.99

Scenes and Monologues from Steinberg/ATCA New Play Award Finalists, 2008-2012
edited by Bruce Burgun
9781476868783 ....$19.99

Soliloquy!
The Shakespeare Monologues
edited by Michael Earley and Philippa Keil
9780936839783 Men's Edition.......$12.99
9780936839790 Women's Edition..$14.95

Teen Boys' Comedic Monologues That Are Actually Funny
edited by Alisha Gaddis
9781480396791 ....$14.99

Teen Girls' Comedic Monologues That Are Actually Funny
edited by Alisha Gaddis
9781480396807 ....$14.99

Women's Comedic Monologues That Are Actually Funny
edited by Alisha Gaddis
9781480360426............................$14.99

APPLAUSE
THEATRE & CINEMA BOOKS
AN IMPRINT OF
HAL•LEONARD®
www.halleonardbooks.com

More Acting Titles from Applause

The Best Plays from American Theater Festivals, 2015
edited by John Patrick Bray
9781495057748...............$19.99

5-Minute Plays
edited by Lawrence Harbison
9781495069246...............$16.99

5-Minute Plays for Teens
edited by Lawrence Harbison
9781495069253...............$16.99

How I Did It
Establishing a Playwriting Career
edited by Lawrence Harbison
9781480369634...............$24.99

25 10-Minute Plays for Teens
edited by Lawrence Harbison
9781480387768...............$16.99

More 10-Minute Plays for Teens
edited by Lawrence Harbison
9781495011801...............$9.99

10-Minute Plays for Kids
edited by Lawrence Harbison
9781495053399...............$9.99

The Monologue Audition
A Practical Guide for Actors
by Karen Kohlhaas
9780879102913...............$22.99

The Scene Study Book
Roadmap to Success
by Bruce Miller
9780879103712...............$16.99

Acting Solo
Roadmap to Success
by Bruce Miller
9780879103750...............$16.99

On Singing Onstage
by David Craig
9781557830432...............$18.99

The Stanislavsky Technique: Russia
by Mel Gordon
9780936839080...............$16.95

Speak with Distinction
by Edith Skinner/Revised with New Material Added by Timothy Monich and Lilene Mansell
9781557830470...............$39.99

Recycling Shakespeare
by Charles Marowitz
9781557830944...............$14.95

Actor's Alchemy
Finding the Gold in the Script
by Bruce Miller
9780879103835...............$16.99

Stella Adler—The Art of Acting
compiled & edited by Howard Kissel
9781557833730...............$29.99

Acting in Film
by Michael Caine
9781557832771...............$19.99

The Actor and the Text
by Cicely Berry
9781557831385...............$22.99

The Craftsmen of Dionysus
by Jerome Rockwood
9781557831552...............$19.99

A Performer Prepares
by David Craig
9781557833952...............$19.99

Directing the Action
by Charles Marowitz
9781557830722...............$19.99

Acting in Restoration Comedy
by Simon Callow
9781557831194...............$18.99

The Shakespeare Audition
How to Get Over Your Fear, Find the Right Piece, and Have a Great Audition
by Laura Wayth
9781495010804...............$16.99

The Young Actor's Handbook
by Jeremy Kruse
9781495075421...............$12.99

Accents
A Manual for Actors – Revised & Expanded Edition
by Robert Blumenfeld
9780879109677...............$29.99

Acting with the Voice
The Art of Recording Books
by Robert Blumenfeld
9780879103019...............$19.95

Workshopping the New Play
A Guide for Playwrights, Directors, and Dramaturgs
by George Sapio
9781495088223...............$16.99

The Best American Short Plays 2015-2016
edited by William W. Demastes and John Patrick Bray
9781495065408...............$19.99

The Best Plays of 2015
edited by Lawrence Harbison
9781495045813...............$19.99

The Richard Wesley Play Anthology
by Richard Wesley
9781480394995...............$19.99

APPLAUSE
THEATRE & CINEMA BOOKS
AN IMPRINT OF
HAL•LEONARD
www.halleonardbooks.com

Prices, contents, and availability subject to change without notice.